andrei dvoretski
RED SEA DIVE GUIDE

Dive-guide
on the best dive-sites
of the reef systems Saint-Johns,
Fury Shoal, Marsa Alam, include
Elphinestoun, and off-shore
marine parks Brothers, Daedalus,
Zabargad and Rocky
80 pages + cover

All right reserved. No part of this book may be reproduced or transmitted in any form or by any means, electronic or mechanical, including photocopying, recording or by any information storage retrieval system, without permission from autor.
Andrei Dvoretski © 2008

andrei dvoretski
red se
dive-gui

on the best dive-sites
of the reefs systems:
saint-johns,
fury shoal,
marsa alam,
include
elphinestoun
and off-shore
marine parks:
brothers,
daedalus,
zabargad
and rocky

2008

EGYPT, RED SEA
mob. +2 010 632 0096
e-mail: info@r-divers.ru
web: www.r-divers.ru

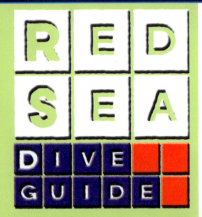

In this book there is one of the possible variants of 10 days safari with the visiting of the most remote places of diving in the Southern part of Egypt, which is rare enough. This is the most interesting rout, with duration of 10 days and extending of about 1000 km, during which one has an opportunity to make dives on the most different sites.

More than 30 of them are represented here with comments and characteristics, including their coordinates and places of boats' moorings. In the describable part also the typical variants of dives on these reefs are given.

In 2008 the continuation of this series is prepared for release: «Reefs of the systems St. Johns and Fury Shoal» and «Reefs of Marsa Alam, Wadi Gimal and Hamata's area»

The safaris on southern reefs of the Egyptian part of Red sea are very popular. The overwhelming majority of safari-tours during last years are really «southern». Nevertheless, I could not find the certain source, which could give the participants the necessary minimum of the information about the diving places. For this reason there was an idea of creation of this guidebook. During years I have collected many maps, schemes, contours, which concern exactly these places. The information about the most interesting and picturesque reefs and sites is selected for this guidebook. This release is dedicated to dive-sites for 10 days' safari «Great Islands Tour», which main idea is to visit Remote Island – national parks and to meet reef systems St. Johns and Fury Shoal. In the guidebook the majority of shore, coastal reefs, which are acceptable during dives from the shore in a mode «daily», except only these reefs, which are visited also during one and two days safari-tours, are not described.

The area called «Far South» or «Deep South» covers dive sites from the small town of Quseir down to the border with Sudan. The vast size of this area, and also the fact that many of these sites have only been recently discovered over the last three to four years, mean that many of them have no settled names. Captains of safari boats, often former fishermen, named the reefs to the tourists in any possible way. Each fleet, and even each boat, had their own names. For example, one of the Egyptian guides that I worked with for about one and a half years,

called the reefs of Saint Johns - «Wahed», «Etneen», «Talata», i.e. he named them by numbers (one-two-three...), according to their remoteness from the island of Zabargad.

As time goes on and people communicate, those names which are less frequently used are replaced by more common ones. So, for example, the last reef of this area in the program of this guide has been named «Saint Johns - Setta», that means «sixth». Gradually it has become more popularly known as Caves, and «Umm Khararim» (Arabian «Mother of Caves»).

The current names of the majority of the reefs may sound exotic, but are frequently very simple. If you remember the translation of a few Arabic words, you can easily name an unknown reef, or define your whereabouts.

Abu - an indefinite article meaning belonging to a male ancestor (something like «father»), unlike Umm - the same, but a female (usually translated as «mother» in the meaning of «foremother»)

Arug (El Arouk, Umm El Arouk) – reef-turret, column

Erg - almost the same, as Arouk, but larger. It is an actual small reef.

Fanous - a light, lighthouse

Gezirat (Geziret, Gezira) - island

Gota (Gotha) - a piece, a part of something.

Habili - small reef, with a top not reaching the surface of the water for 3-4m.

Kebir – big (male). Kebira – big (female).

Marsa - a bay with mooring.
Ras - the cape, a part of a reef which is moved out to the sea or land
Sha'ab – valuable separately detached reef
Sha'abrur - almost the same, but with the indication that nearby there is a more significant place. (e.g. Sha'abrur Umm Gamar, «a reef near to Umm Gamar»)
Sharm - a bay, a gulf.
Sogayar (Soraya, Sagir), - small.
Torfa - not an independent reef but a part of something greater, e.g. an island
Tobia - the Tower, Donjon.
Wadi - area of a channel of a dried-up river

The dictionary is not big and not full, but these words are quite enough for identification of the most of places.

When a reef gets its name, it is usually given a brief classification («sha'ab», «arouk», «habili», «gota», «marsa», «ras») and assigned to a territory («Marsa Alam», «Saint Johns», «Wadi Gimal»). Sometimes an extra definition in the form of a typical peculiarity of this reef («sogayar», «kebir»), or above-water mark («fanous») is added.

So, for example, the name Sha'ab Marsa Alam tells you that it is the big reef (Sha'ab), located to a bay of the certain Alam (Marsa Alam) nearby. And Saint Johns Gota Kebir is a certain part (gota), which is greater (kebir) than one more part, located nearby, which is smaller (Gota Sogayar).

Now you can learn a lot about a reef only because of its name even if for any reasons you will not have this edition. Having learned,

it is necessary to dive and see. And it is better to dive on a safari.

The most right period for a safari on «South» - ten days. For this time it is possible to visit the majority of «cult» places of this extensive area. And the sensation of that all has already ended, hardly having begun, is not so sharp, as on a week safari. Usually this route is called «Great Islands Tour».

It is the first release of the Guidebook. Certainly in it there will be typing errors and inaccuracies. Something interesting can be passed, or is indicated not absolutely correctly. I shall be grateful to receive any remarks and amendments, for to the next edition will be «corrected and modified» and will be really useful for everyone who will dive, being collated with its advices and the help. Therefore send your remarks, wishes and offers on e-mail info@r-divers.ru with a mark «guidebook».

Meet you on safari and pages of the present and next guidebooks.

Wish you an equal quantity of dives and coming on surface.

I thank everyone who helped me with preparation of this edition.

Andrei
DVORETSKI

Red Sea
Egypt

2008

Pages on the Guide:
Marsa Alam area:
Port Ghalib	05-06
Marsa Shona	07-08
Sha'ab Marsa Alam	09-10
Ras Torombi	11-12
Sha'ab Sharm	67-70
Elphinestoun	71-74
Abu Dabbab	75-76

Marine parks:
Small Brother Island	15-20
Big Brother Island	21-26
Daedalus	27-28
Rocky Island	29-34
Zabargad Island	35-38

Saint Johns area:
Habili Ali	41-42
Habili Gafar	43-44
Abu Bassala	45-46
Dangerous	47-48
Gota Kebir	49-50
Gota Sogayar	51-52
Caves	53-54
Mikauwa Island	55-56

Fury Shoal area:
Sha'ab Maksour	59-60
Sha'ab Claudia	61-62
El Malahi	63-64
Abu Galava	65-66

Additional info:
HEPCA & RSDASS	77
Useful phone & DECO int.	78

The program of the Great Islands Tour*

1st day
Port Ghalib	05-06
Marsa Shoona	07-08
Sha'ab Marsa Alam	09-10
Ras Torombi	11-12
Sailing to Brothers Islands (84 km)	

2nd day
Small Brother – Northeast	17-18
Small Brother – Southwest	19-20
Small Brother – Southwest plateau	21-22

3rd day
Big Brother – East point	21-22
Big Brother – Numidia wreck	23-24
Big Brother – Aida wreck	25-26
Sailing to Daedalus (175 km)	

4th day
Daedalus Reef – Northeast	27-28
Daedalus Reef – Southeast	27-28
Daedalus Reef – Northwest	27-28
Sailing to Rocky Island (159 km)	

5th day
Rocky Island	29-30
Rocky Island – Southwest	31-32
Rocky Island – Northeast	33-34
Zabargad Island – South	35-36

6th day
Zabargad Island	37-38
Sailing to St. John's area (30 km)	
Habili Ali	41-42
Habili Gafar	43-44
Abu Bassala	45-46

* To participation in this safari it is necessary to have sufficient experience of diving. Egyptian legislation defines this as 50 logged dives at the beginning of the tour.

on days and pages of the Guidebook:

7th day
Gota Kebir	49-50
Gota Sogayar	51-52
Umm Hararym (Caves)	53-54
Mikauwa Island	55-56
Sailing to Fury Shoal (53 km)	

8th day
Sha'ab Maksour	59-60
Sha'ab Claudia	61-62
El Malahi	63-64
Abu Galava	65-66
Sailing to Sha'ab Sharm (85 km)	67-70

9th day
Sailing to Elphinestoun (67 km)	
Elphinstoun North	71-72
Elphinstoun South	73-74
Abu Dabbab	75-76
Returning in Port Ghalib	

** This is just one of the possible variants of the «Great Islands Tour». The main sites visited are the islands, which are part of the state nature protection zone «Marine Park», - the islands of the Brothers, Rocky and Zabargad, and the reef Daedalus. The choice of reefs of the systems Saint Johns and Fury Shoal is defined by preferences of the group and also by weather conditions (see page 67). Similarly, the selection of reefs for the first and last days of the safari is dependent on the port of departure. For example, this tour can begin in Hurghada and finish in Port Ghalib. For this variant, the choice of reefs on the first day will be limited to the reefs of Hurghada and Safaga (not included in this guidebook).

Copyright © 2007 Andrei DVORETSKI www.r-divers.ru

port ghalib

alternative names:
marsa galib, port ghaleb

Location:
320 km on the South from Hurghada, 50 km. on the North from Marsa Alam.

Co-ordinates (GPS - position):
25°28'10.28" N 34°40'57.33" E
(Harbourmaster office)

More information:

phone	+2 065 370 0240
fax	+2 065 370 0241
mob	+2 010 343 4708

web: portghalibmarina.com
e-mail: marina@portghalib.com

New international Port Ghalib is the beginning of all routes including the reefs and islands of the National Park of Egypt.

The harbour of 5m depth can accept boats up to 50m long and provides mooring and all necessary facilities and supplies including fuel, electricity, fresh water and Internet connection. The port is considerably built up. It consists of an international conferences centre with a festival hall, hotels and a complex of shops, galleries, cafes, restaurants and bars.

Operation of the port began in April 2002, six months after the opening of Marsa Alam airport in October 2001. The airport is situated opposite the port just 5km away. Today the airport receives weekly flights from the UK, Germany, Italy, France and Switzerland, and also from Cairo International Airport. These modern transport units account for the huge influx of tourists who are spending their holidays in the rapidly developing resort conglomerate of Marsa Alam.

A significant number of those arriving here are scuba divers, coming to dive the southern reefs of the Egyptian Red Sea. Port Ghalib is not only the base for an extensive fleet of safari boats, but also accepts boats from New Zealand, Spain, Germany, Croatia and the UK.

Annually from Port Ghalib about 500 dive safaris are carried out, mostly to Marine Parks of Egypt – Daedalus Reef, Brother Islands, and the islands of Zabargad and Rocky.

RED SEA DIVING SAFARI

R-DIVERS.RU

Red Sea, EGYPT
+2 0114 364 1166
info@r-divers.ru
www.r-divers.ru

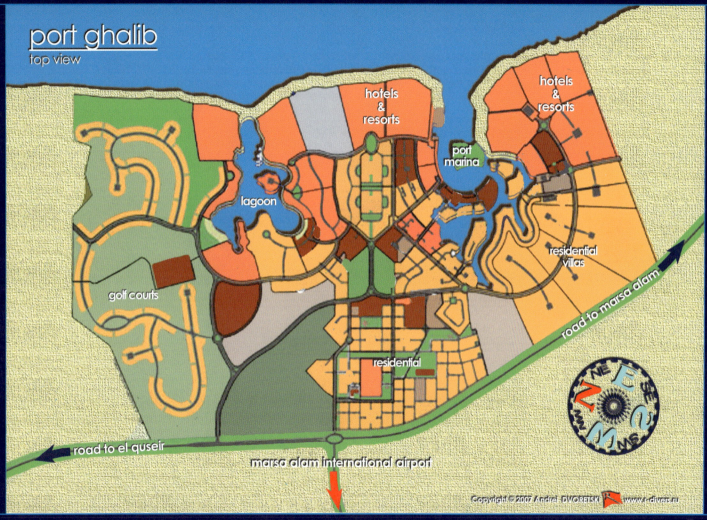

marsa shoona

alternative names:
marsa shony, el shona

Location:
9,2 km. on south from Port Ghalib, 50 km from Marsa Alam. Coastal bay

GPS - position:
25°28'10.28" N
34°40'57.33" E

Access:
Car
Daily boat
Safari

Mooring:
South and southeast part of the bay.

Recommended level:
CMAS * / PADI OWD

Average depth
12.0 m.

Maximum depth
25 m.

Current
Weak

Visibility
Good (10-20 m)

Type of dives
- Check
- Entry
- Rreef
- Night

The first part of the name of this site (Marsa) in translation with Arabic means «bay». It is not really a big coastal cove, more a bay in a coral coastal barrier. There are many such bays along the whole coast and all of them are quite similar. As a rule, each Marsa is a superficial bay, well protected from prevailing northern winds and bordered by a coral wall. The depth at the base of the wall is typically 10-12m and, usually, there is a deeper «external» northern part. These bays are ideal places for check dives and night moorings.

The recommended entry point into the water is about 150m from a corner of the northern part of the lagoon, 15-30m away from the reef wall. Here, at depths up to 18m you find fine coral sand with rare corals and «table coral» acropora.

Having dropped down to one of the sandy bottom areas, this is the perfect place to practice skills. Here you can recall how to find and clear your regulator, clear your mask and, the main thing, to control buoyancy. Then, moving in a north-easterly direction, passing scattered coral formations, you gradually approach the main reef. With a little more than 100 bar in your tank, you can turn and keep close to the reef on your right side. The depth here at the bottom of the reef is from 12-6m. The wall of hard porous corals with acropora at the base is very picturesque. The reef is well lit and occupied by various creatures including huge moray and blue spotted sting rays, napoleon, green turtles and even white-tip reef sharks.

You finish your dive here whilst continuing to explore part of the reef wall at a depth of 5m, doing your safety stop whilst you move along, perfecting your buoyancy.

Emperor angelfish. Marsa Shoona. A. Shestopalets 2005

There is almost no current here. The contrary current is possible at the approach to the northeast corner of the reef and on the external east wall. Being a half-bordered coastal reef, sometimes Shona has poor visibility. However, on the «external» northern wall of the bay you can find both strong currents and extremely clear waters.

Good place for the first dive on a safari from Port Ghalib. This site offers both sandy «lawns» below the moorings and an internal reef wall with good colonies of hard and soft corals. The main reef creatures are stingrays. There are also turtles.

sha'ab marsa alam

alternative names: marsa alam reef

Location:
66 km to South from Port Ghalib. 18 km from Marsa Alam.
Co-ordinates (GPS - position):
25° 04'54.51" N
35° 03'51.21" E
Access:
Daily boat
Safari
Mooring:
Internal part of east site of a reef.
Recommended level:
CMAS * / PADI OWD
Average depth:
14.0 m
Maximum depth:
30 m
Current:
Weak
Visibility:
Good (15-25 m)
Type of dives
- Cavern
- Reef
- Night

After the check dive at Marsa Shona, it is possible to move a little to the southwest, to reef Sha'ab Marsa Alam. This place is close enough to make a full dive, followed by a night dive, and then at night to continue onto the Brother Islands.

This reef is big, curved to the north, and forms a very quiet bay on the internal southern side. The most interesting parts of the reef for diving are the east, southeast, external wall and a southwest part of the reef bay. This is also the mooring point for the boats.

If you have enough time for two dives then it is best to make the first dive on the external northeast part of the reef whilst there is enough light. Having reached your maximum planned depth, keep the reef to the right shoulder and move to the south gradually coming to the surface. Here there can be quite a good passing current which makes movement easier and provides excellent visibility. Cornet fish, jackfish, trevally and barracudas will accompany you. Boulders of hard porous corals go down from the wall to the bottom, forming below and to the left of the reef an extensive coral garden. Several partially destroyed coral lie close to the southern extreme. Here you can meet dolphins and the first sharks of your trip.

Following along the reef wall, as you turn to the west you reach the mooring point. The dive ends at the internal reef wall in a lagoon. Here many pillar-like corals give shelter to blue spotted sting rays, morays, lionfish and groupers. There is almost no current.

To the left of the mooring, the small pyramidal reef is almost split into two unequal parts by a canyon at 8-9 m. In the southern part of this reef there is a small cave swim-through. It curves a little but is quite wide enough to comfortably and safely pass through.

Here at the bottom of the northwest slope of the reef, at a depth of 10-12m lies a safari boat that sunk three years ago. The wreck is around 30m in length and lies on its right side. The two main decks are completely destroyed. However, the hull is completely safe, opening to two passages leading to the blocks of cabins (four cabins in each) in which even the toilets remain. A part of the deck above the engine room is open and one can see engines and generators populated by swarms of glassfish. A giant grouper watches from the corner. Other parts of the superstructure and boat equipment are scattered around.

The whole lagoon is boarded from the east and the north by a reef wall, and from the west by a reef-pyramid and the remains of the sunken boat - an excellent place for night diving.

Blue spotted stingray. Sha'am Marsa Alam. A. Shestopalets 2005

The reef is located near to Marsa Alam and, rather nearby, from Port Galib, therefore very often is a place of the first, or last days a safari. Well closed mooring. The coral garden on an external wall is good for day dives, and shallow lagoon with the sunk yacht and a turret with a cave, - very good for night dive.

ras torombi

ras toromby, torombi cape

After the check dive in Marsa Shona and dives on reef Sha'ab Marsa Alam, there is time to make evening and night dives.

You and the captain of your boat have a choice - to remain until the end of the day on Abu Dabbab or to move a little to the north, to the bay Toromby, reducing the distance to the Brother Islands. The bay (Marsa Toromby) is not so different from Shona but it has a remarkable feature - a cape, or headland on the west, known as Ras Toromby. If the route of your safari returns to Port Ghalib after diving the Brothers, the visit to this reef can be postponed as it's better to dive here in the first half of the day. By the evening, unfortunately this reef is already partly in shadow. The corals and all the creatures will appear grey and pale. Despite this, the structure of the site is such that even with insufficient illumination, you cannot dislike the diving.

Heading out into the sea, the cape is not a monolith. It is cut through with canyons, filled by separate turrets and reminds you of a wall of a rather fantastic castle or fortress, with entrances, balconies and terraces. It is possible to enter this «castle» and here you will see small «halls» open from above and with sets of entrances and «windows».

A weak northern current provides excellent visibility and numerous corals; and the main thing, lots of corners to "chill-out". This is the home of various reef creatures, everything from a glassfish to stingrays and scorpion fish. Typical of the majority of coastal reefs, green turtles are also not a rarity. Look in the grottoes and caves to spot small white tip reef sharks.

It is better to begin the dive from a «zodiac» which will take you out on the northwest wall. Having turned your right shoulder to the reef wall, you can drift with the passing current, investigating corners of this unusual place, gradually heading back to the mooring.

At the end of the dive inside the bay, you can look around for a suitable spot for a night dive. This will be much more interesting than a dive in the evening due to the game of light and shadow from the torches on whimsically cut-up surfaces of the hard and soft coral walls, and an abundance of new, night inhabitants.

Arabian boxfish. Ras Torombi. A. Shestopalets 2005

Location:
15,5 km. on the North from Port Galib. Northern cape of a Marsa Toromby coastal bay.

Co-ordinates (GPS - position):
25°39'44.60" N
34°35'8.81"B E

Access:
Car, Daily boat
Safari

Mooring:
100-150 metres to the West from east site of a reef. All northern part of a bay.

Recommended level:
CMAS * / PADI OWD

Average depth
14.0 m.

Maximum depth:
18 m.

Current:
Weak

Visibility:
Good (15-25 m)

Type of dives:
- Reef
- Night

The perfect end point of the first day of a dive safari to the Brother Islands from Port Ghalib.

The structure of the reef is very picturesque and there are a lot of pyramids of porous coral, especially on the northern and northeast extremities of the main reef, which expands in a direction of the open sea and therefore creates internal lagoons.

brothers islands

alternative names:
el akhawein gezirat

Location:
In the open sea, 88 km on the northeast from Port Ghalib.

76,5 km on the northeast from Ras Torombi cape.

GPS - position:
26°18'7.32" N; 34°51'44.34" E
26°18'6.87" N; 34°50'8.05" E

Access:
Safari from Hurghada or Port Ghalib

Mooring:
South site of the Small Brother and south coast of the Big Brother Island

Recommended level:
CMAS ** / PADI AOWD

Average depth:
30 m

Maximum depth:
More than 100 m

Current:
Strong (more than 2 knots)

Visibility:
Good (25-30 m)

Type of dives:
- Wall, Deep, Drift, Wreck

Requirements to divers:
- Minimal experience - 50 logged (registered) dives
- Presence of the surface marker-buoy (SMB) - each diver
- Presence of a light source (in the day time) - one per pair
- Presence a marker-buoy, a light source, and an additional alarm device, for example, a heliograph - the dive-guide.
- Support of local dive guides - one guide per 8 persons

Two small islands, Big Brother and Little Brother, are surrounded on the perimeter by a barrier reef. Actually, these islands are the two tops of one mountain, which has arisen as a result of volcanic activity. The bottom of the «mountain» lies several hundreds of metres deep in the open sea. The underwater part connecting the two tops forms a ridge, which rises from the depths to around 70m. The steep slopes flatten out to a depth of 175m and bottom out into a valley at around 375m.

These reefs are unique in their location. The isolated position of the islands and their openness to winds, waves and currents creates unique conditions for the formation of colonies of all kinds of corals, and also for all forms of the living creatures connected with these corals.

Taking these circumstances into account, the Egyptian authorities have given these islands the status of National Marine Park. Visiting boats must have special certifications and an additional permission for each excursion to the islands themselves. These Marine Park tickets are issued for divers and non-divers alike.

Bewitching landscapes, steep slopes covered by fantastic corals, the high probability to see sharks and other pelagic and reef predators... you will understand why these islands are so attractive.

Strong underwater and surface currents are usual here and must be considered. Each diver should carry an SMB and be able to use it.

Do not leave the walls – the speed and direction of the current is very unpredictable. It is possible to lose reference points very easily, which is extremely dangerous in the open sea.

Lighthouse on Big Brother Island

small brother

alternative names: el akhawein sogayar

This oval island extends on an axis from south to north-northwest and is approximately 180m x 100m with a small beach. A reef plateau surrounds the island at a width of between 50m-100m at the surface. The northern part of the plateau gradually goes underwater to a depth of 5-6m over about 100m distance. On the northern extremity of the reef, at a depth of 42-45m there is a ledge, something like a small plateau, with the diameter of about 5m, placed exactly at the division of current on two streams - the east and western walls of the reef.

This plateau is one of the best places in Egypt for observing sharks. Here it is possible to meet small groups of grey sharks and also silvertip reef sharks. Once divers make an appearance on the plateau, curious hammerhead sharks frequently swim up for closer examination of the newcomers, before disappearing into the blue that surrounds the plateau.

If the current allows, after visiting the northern plateau, it is best to continue to dive along the east wall of Little Brother. The forest of Gorgonian fans begins at 40m depth and rises almost to the surface. This is a true forest that covers many tens of metres of reef slope. Here you can relax in the drift of the current and look at the right side as the forest of Gorgonian is replaced by plentiful bushes of black corals, and splendid red, pink and blue soft corals that serve as a refuge for small fry of numerous colours and sizes. On the left side, tuna, huge barracudas, sharks and sometimes a manta float gracefully by.

The second dive needs to be made before dinner while the sun still lights up the east slope. It is possible to begin it in the same place, above the northern plateau, but it's better to start early in the hope to catch the sharks that you observed in the morning. Keeping the reef to the right side, you can enjoy all kinds of corals, which punctuate the almost vertical reef slopes with colour. Most often, this dive follows the current to finish at the southern plateau and the mooring. When planning the dive, a short opposite current should be considered which often covers the relatively short distance of 15-20m and is quite easily overcome. Try not to use too much strength here and stick closer to the walls and seek protection in its many ledges. If the current is too strong, then the dive should be aborted, especially if you have drifted from the reef wall.

It is best to start the evening dive at a distance of 50m-100m to the south of the northern plateau, on the western wall. After noon, this part of the reef is perfected illuminated and you can rest in the weak passing current. The southern plateau is not like the northern; a significant wide ledge begins on the western slope and surrounds the whole southern part of the reef, coming to an end on the east slope. The plateau is not whole, but consists of rocky and coral ledges on depths ranging from 20m to 45m. It is an ideal place to end the evening dive. In the blue near the plateau one can see sharks rising at this time almost up to the surface where shoals of tuna and barracuda continue to circle. This plateau is quite suitable for a separate dive, which you can often begin directly from the dive deck of your boat. By swimming above the plateau, it is possible to change direction from east to west and rise along the southern wall of the reef.

In the morning, it's possible once again to devote the first dive to meetings with sharks on the northern plateau before heading to Big Brother.

Location:
In the open sea, 88 km. on the northeast from Port Ghalib. 76,5 km on the northeast from Ras Torombi cape.

GPS - position:
26°18'6.87" N; 34°50'8.05" E

Access:
Safari from Hurghada or Port Ghalib

Mooring:
South site of the Island

Recommended level:
CMAS ** / PADI AOWD

Average depth:
30 m.

Maximum depth:
More than 100 m.

Current:
Strong (more than 2 knots)

Visibility:
Good (25-30 m.)

Type of dives:
- Reef wall
- Drift
- Deep

Here is the best place in Egypt for observing sharks at the northern plateau of the reef. Take care - here there are often very strong currents of a variable direction.

The reef is so beautiful and rich with corals and living creatures that it is possible to dive here for two or even three days. Night dives are not allowed.

giant moray
M. Ustinova 2007

reef shark (little brother)
A. Shestopalets 2006

big brother

alternative names:
el akhawein kebir

Location:
In the open sea, 88 km. on the northeast from Port Ghalib, About 1,5 km on the northwest from Small Brother Island.

Co-ordinates (GPS - position):
26°18'7.32" N; 34°51'44.34" E

Access:
Safari from Hurghada or Port Ghalib

Mooring:
Southeast coast

Recommended level:
CMAS ** / PADI AOWD

Average depth:
40 m

Maximum depth:
More than 100 m.

Current:
Strong (more than 2 knots)

Visibility:
Good (25-30 m)

Type of dives:
- Reef wall
- Drift
- Deep
- Wreck

The reef slope here is nearly vertical rather than a soft incline. Constant currents bring plankton-rich water to feed the numerous kinds of coral. Soft corals of red, claret and blue-violet colours begin at depths of 5-6m and cover the reef walls to more than 40 m.

On the southeast extremity of the island there is an extensive plateau located at 35-40m. This plateau is a fine place for shark observation. Here it is possible to meet not only habitual grey reef sharks, but also rare and larger silvertip reef sharks. Shoals of barracuda and jackfish are also usual here. If stocks of air and non-decompression limits allow it is great to look out into the blue at the edge of the plateau to find large pelagic predators; not only tuna, but also hammerhead sharks. Moving ahead with the current in a western direction (reef on the right hand), it is possible to see how the plateau is again replaced by vertical walls decorated with soft corals and huge Gorgonians. Small holes in the walls, especially close to the surface, give shelter for numerous small fry. Overhangings often become small caves, filled by glassfish and sweepers (Yellow sweeper, Dusky sweeper). It is best to spot the larger reef inhabitants on the very first dive, soon after dawn. At this particular time, meetings with the thresher sharks, who are constant inhabitants of the reef, are frequent.

At least three dives may be made here in order to get acquainted with the island. As on Little Brother, night dives are strictly forbidden. The main sights of Big Brother are two shipwrecks lying on its southwest slopes. The English cargo boat Numidia, sank in July 1901, whose hull lays on an abrupt slope, at a depth of 7m down to 80m, and the Egyptian transport boat Aida, which sank in September 1957 and lies at 30-68m. The remains of the boats are so overgrown with corals that they have become one and the same with the reef.

Longimanus. Big Brother. A. Shestopalets 2005

The lighthouse was constructed by the company Chance Bros. of Birmingham in the 80th years of the 19th century. In 1994 modern lighting devices, accumulators and solar batteries were established. An excursion to the lighthouse and a trip up the spiral staircase to a viewing platform is usually included in the program of a safari.

numidia wreck

alternative names: nuweiba wreck

This British cargo ship was constructed in Glasgow at the beginning of 1901. At 137.4m long and 16.7m wide, the displacement was more than 6000 tons. The engine, a three-cylinder steam machine, allowed the ship to develop a speed of 10 knots. On February 28th 1901 Numidia left Glasgow for its last campaign. Numidia bore a cargo in weight of about 7000 tons and 97 crew members. There were no passengers.

On July 19th 1901 at 02:10 in the morning, the boat ran aground on a reef-surrounded island, right opposite a lighthouse... After two hours of attempts to remove the boat from a rock, the engines were stopped. The crew were all saved and during the seven weeks that followed, the majority if the cargo was taken off before the ship was finally sunk. On the conclusion of the commission, the reason for the accident was stated as the officer of the watch had fallen asleep on a post.

The stern part of the boat is mostly destroyed and its hull starts from a depth of around 8m. This part of the dive is significant for two big locomotive wheels that were transported as deck cargo. From here down, the hull is less destroyed and keeps the initial form.

The main thing that divers comment on here is the magnificent set of coloured soft and hard corals that the colonized the boat and transformed it into one of the most beautiful shipwrecks in the world. Rails, masts, boat davits of life boats, cables and winches of the deck which are all still in place have become a part of a living reef to such a degree that it is easy to forget that the basis of this colony is an artificial construction. Even those who do not like to dive wrecks will be compelled to recognize that this «piece of ironmongery» is now an absolutely fantastic coral, multi-coloured formation that is occupied by many reef creatures controlled by huge groupers.

Despite the lost wooden parts, and the saved cargo, there are still plenty of places to explore. In front of the central bridge there are two cargo bunkers with ventilating hatches on the right. The wooden deck covering is lost and starting from the first mast, rectangular designs of an iron skeleton are naked. Right behind the second mast are located the rest of the central «lock» where the captain's bridge settled down earlier. Being a wooden construction on a steel structure, the whole bridge is destroyed, except for the main metal designs of a skeleton and the platform of a floor. The depth here is already about 50m and any further exploration of the remains of the boat is possible only with the application of technical means.

Right behind the bridge, the pipe of the steam machine has fallen on one side. Here are several boat davits for life boats and an engine section. Further, behind the rests of the 3rd and 4th masts, there are some remains of a stern mast and deck winches. The border of the round stern deck is also well intact, as well as the unique big rowing screw at a depth of more than 90m.

The dive here should be made from a zodiac. One should start the dive as close as possible to the reef and a little bit further north so that the current assists your descent. Having seen the hull, dive along the length of the ship at your planned depth and then begin your ascent above the deck as it inclines to the right, well protected from the current. When you finish your exploration of the wreck, it's possible to drift with the current onto the reef where there is a good ledge at 15-25m. Here you can check your air before gradually ascending towards the mooring. The reef walls lies to your left. As a rule, there is a weak passing current. Just 100m away, you can see on the right, in the depths, the second object - the wreck of the transport ship Aida, the focus of your other dive here.

Location:
Reef slope on east site of Island

Co-ordinates (GPS - position):
26°18'7.32" N; 34°51'44.34" E (co-ordinates of Lighthouse)

Access:
Safari from Hurghada or Port Ghalib

Mooring:
South coast

Recommended level:
CMAS ** / PADI AOWD

Average depth:
30 m.

Maximum depth:
More than 100 m.

Current:
Strong (more than 2 knots)

Visibility:
Good (25-30 m)

Type of dives:
- Reef wall
- Drift
- Deep
- Wreck

Numidia - the English transport ship, which ran aground on the reef and sank at Big Brother Island at the beginning of the 20th century, more than one hundred years ago. Now it is an absolutely fantastic multi-coloured coral 'reef', occupied by many different living creatures controlled by huge groupers.

At the beginning of the dive there is the fine opportunity to observe sharks and hammerheads.

aida wreck

alternative names: aida-2 wreck

Aida is the transport supply ship of the lighthouse that sank in 1957. The remains of the boat lie on a steep slope and the hull and superstructure are so covered in soft and hard corals that they resemble a strangely trimmed bush rather than pieces of metal.

Aida was constructed and launched in France in 1911 under the order of the Egyptian Administration of Ports and Lighthouses. The length of the ship was 75m and its width 9.7m. Displacement was 1400 tons. A 3 cylinder engine allowed a developing speed of 9 knots.

There is a mention of this boat in the British War Diary from October 8th 1941. It mentions the transport ship Aida being torpedoed whilst lying at anchor nearby to the settlement Zafrana, by a bomber of the German "Luftwaffe". Owing to the fast actions of the captain, the ship did not sink but was run aground. It was then restored and re-launched on the water. Probably for this reason it is sometimes called Aida-2.

On September 15th 1957 the captain of Aida took the ship to Big Brother to supply provisions and fresh water. A strong storm was raging and as the captain tried to manoeuvre for mooring, he struck a rock and the ship began to sink immediately. The captain and 77 members of the crew were urgently evacuated by a small towboat. Aida drifted for sometime along the reef to the west, up to the moment when its nose once again struck the reef. The boat broke apart and under an abrupt corner went astern under the water and finally sank.

Now the boat lies almost vertically at a depth of 30m down to at least 60m at the stern. The hull of the boat is practically not damaged except for the stern part, which was destroyed against the reef. Wooden parts have only disappeared over time. The metal hull and construction has become covered by dense soft and hard corals over the last 50 years. The wreck has become a natural and very picturesque part of the reef colony of Big Brother, densely occupied by living creatures. The forward hold is empty and protects the diver from strong currents.

The first mast is well kept. Below the mast, there is a set of winches and a beam lying across the deck. In the middle of the boat there is a raised platform of the central bridge with the rest of a metal skeleton of this construction. In many cabins, copper windows and other details of equipment are still intact. The pipe of a boat is situated at 50m and is deeply rusted. There is also the massive steam whistle, very similar to the whistle from the Rosalie Moeller. Here there is also an entrance to the engine room where the 3 cylinder steam machine is situated. To the right and below, at a depth of more than 60m is the massive rowing screw.

The stern part is also almost undamaged, except for the decayed wooden parts, and is considerably overgrown with corals for such depths. Here one can meet the greatest groupers of the Red Sea.

The dive begins a little to the west of the fragments scattered on a slope. A relatively fast descent to the boat follows, taking in the places most protected from the current. As you ascend back towards the mooring, you return along the reef wall on your left shoulder. The best place to end the dive is the well-protected small lagoon, lying at the foot of the lighthouse. Part of the jetty is underwater and makes a good reference point. The safety stop offers you a meeting with a napoleon fish and even a big green turtle. In the distance, less than 100m to the west from Aida, one can see a much older boat, which sank right at the beginning of the 20th century - the SS Numidia.

Location:
Big Brother Island: Reef slope on southeast site, About 150 metres from east extremity of Island.

Co-ordinates (GPS - position):
26°18'7.32" N; 34°51'44.34" E
(co-ordinates of Lighthouse)

Access:
Safari from Hurghada or Port Ghalib

Mooring:
South coast

Recommended level:
CMAS **
PADI AOWD

Average depth:
30 m.

Maximum depth:
More than 100 m.

Current:
Strong (more than 2 knots)

Visibility:
Good (25-30 m)

Type of dives:
- Reef wall
- Drift
- Deep
- Wreck

Aida is one of two boats that sank at Big Brother.

Having lain on a slope for more than 50 years already, the hull of this transport ship has become an integral part of the reef. It has become home for many magnificent coral colonies and a refuge for a set of diverse reef life.

daedalus reef

alternative names:
abu el kizan

Location:
147 km. on the southeast from Port Ghalib. From Brothers Islands 176 km. on the south

Co-ordinates (GPS - position):
25° 1'44.54" N;35°53'16.03"" E

Access:
Safari from Port Ghalib

Mooring:
South site

Recommended level:
CMAS ** / PADI AOWD

Average depth:
30 m.

Maximum depth:
More than 100 m.

Current:
Strong (more than 2 knots)

Visibility:
Good (25-30 m)

Type of dives:
- Reef wall
- Deep
- Drift

This rather small reef is situated in the open sea, almost halfway to Saudi Arabia. It is less than 800m in diameter. A lighthouse marks the reef, which is the only thing that towers above the surface for many miles around. The reef slopes are almost vertical and covered in coral colonies that stretch from the surface into the depths. Since the reef is isolated, the virginity of the corals is maintained. The beauty of the corals here is often compared to that of the Brother Islands. The east, north and southeast slopes are most interesting for diving. The southern part also offers protected moorings from the prevailing northern winds. There is a big density and a variety of reef creatures more commonly seen on smaller reefs such as tiny fairy basslets, butterfly fish, dotty-back fishes etc. The usual reef creatures are supplemented with shoals such as tuna, mackerel, trevally and jackfish and many others.

Planning a dive on this reef can appear relatively simple owing to its form and predictability. However, strong currents can make this reef a challenge even for skilled scuba divers. The first dive is usually complex and undertaken on the northern extremities of the reef, whose strong currents practically always guarantee sightings of large predators including sharks and hammerheads. Here, at a depth of 30-35m there is a small ledge in the slightly concave wall of the reef. It's possible to stay here for a while, protected by the side edges of this «balcony» from the strong current, which divides here into two parts, along the east and west slopes. This causes some complexity as short counter-currents form along the length of the angular ledges of the reef. If you do not wish to finish the dive here, you will need to fight a little with the current. Keep as close to the wall as possible and try to move forward with the pulsations of current. Eventually you will make the east wall and can relax here. You should come to the surface only once you are away from the reef some 30m, for surface waves can throw you onto the reef before the zodiac has time to pick you up.

It is better to make the second dive on the east slope. Keeping it on your right side, you can drift along with the passing current to the southern extremity and the mooring point. The slope will be beautifully lit up and you can take pleasure in the majestic beauty of an obvious and impressive wall, which is covered with Gorgonian, soft and hard corals. This way leads to a southeast extremity of the reef where one can meet thresher sharks. You can easily identify them by the extended tails that they use to help «thresh» shoals of smaller fish, stunning them before capturing them to eat.

The third and final dive here is usually made in the afternoon at the western part of the reef. Here, at a depth of 30-40m extends a long plateau to the south and southeast of the reef. On this plateau you will find many "anemone cities" and massive colonies of corals, small coral bushes and separate coral turrets. Moray, stingray and also resident reef sharks are common here. The edges of the plateau, especially its south and southeast part are popular places to watch for pelagic sharks. The passing current will facilitate this dive.

As a rule, one spends one or maximum two days on Daedalus, doing three dives per day. Night dives are forbidden here too for safety reasons.

Owing to the remoteness from the coast and any other dive sites, Daedalus is one of the least visited reefs in Egypt.

The reef itself is insignificant but is the only dwelling place for a considerable distance of lots of living creatures that attract so many large pelagic predators and divers.
A lighthouse on the reef is the native brother of the lighthouse on Big Brother Island. It is also possible to make an excursion here.

rocky island

alternative names: gezirat el gabal

Location:
276 km on the southeast from port Galib. 166,5 km from a Daedalus

Co-ordinates (GPS - position):
23°33'40.02" N; 36°14'40.02" E

Access:
Safari from Port Ghalib

Mooring:
South and southwest coast. There are no night mooring

Recommended level:
CMAS ** / PADI AOWD

Average depth:
30 m.

Maximum depth:
More than 100 m.

Current:
Strong (more than 2 knots)

Visibility:
Good (25-35 m)

Type of dives:
- Reef wall
- Deep
- Drift

This is the most southerly of the islands in the protected natural zone of the «Marine Park» of Egypt. Strong currents guarantee exciting «drifts», tremendous visibility and meetings with sharks. The severe beauty of the walls is so effective, that often this island is preferred to nearby Zabargad, using the latter only as a «base» for mooring and night dives.

Rocky is a very small desert island, approximately 500m by 300m. It is surrounded by a reef plateau between 5-15m wide, the walls plunging downwards to 70-80m. Another plateau, around 100m wide, continues down to depths of around 120m, before dropping into the abyss to over one thousand metres. There is no night diving here, nor the chance of a overnight mooring due to the absence of any protected bays. Even light winds here cause huge waves. A strong northeast current covers the reef from both sides.

North Coast

This part is open to the prevailing northern winds, making a zone of surf along the coastal line, which is sometimes extreme. This dive is absolutely not suitable for beginners and, more often, is impossible directly from a boat. Most likely you will travel by zodiac through surface waves to quieter waters at a corner of the reef to start the dive. Here you can make a fantastic dive at the very abrupt vertical walls. The strong current can make for a fast drift dive and the roughness on the surface can be felt even at significant depths. In some places near to the surface around 8-10m, the water twists and turns in cracks and ledges of the wall as if in a washing machine. The base of the reef is a stone rock with good coral covering, especially at depths up to 20m. In general, the whole northern wall of the reef is covered by soft corals, creating what is probably the best soft coral zone on the island. The fish life is varied with a strong bias to shoaling fish. Reef fish are also well presented, including huge grouper and napoleon. It is possible to see sharks here as with any other part of the island.

South Coast

This is the most protected and therefore the most suitable area for the less skilled. It also offers some of the best coral colonies and reef life. This area is remarkable for its numerous bays, cracks and entrance apertures in the wall of the reef covering all depths. Below the surface, the reef has a practically vertical structure, but is broken by a lot of ledges and grottoes, making a sculptural impression. Corals range from lacy Acropora up to massive Favites and extensive zones of cabbage corals. Soft versions are well distributed, offering unique bushes and big areas in a variety of colours. There are fishes of all forms and sizes, from huge groupers and napoleon, to graceful lionfish. Snapper and sweet lips alternate with humphead parrots, sea angels and butterfly fishes.

East Coast

The coastal coral platforms lead into obvious walls and an open plateau with a strong current. The zodiac will deliver you to the southeast extremity of the island, where you can drift back to the east coast. It is also possible to jump from the mooring point and navigate to the southeast. It is here that meetings with the largest underwater inhabitants of this island are most probable. At a depth of around 25m, a small peak occurs in the reef wall and forms a natural survey platform, «The Shark Theatre». Hanging here, you get an excellent chance to see sharks of all kinds as well as many other exciting creatures. The coral colonies are magnificent and varied, whilst the soft corals are especially beautiful in a coastal bar between the moorings and the southeast corner of the reef.

masked butterflyfish
A. Shestopalets 2008

blue light from a lagoon (zabargad island)
A. Shestopalets 2006

zabargad island

st. johns island, gezirat zabargad

Zabargad Island is where the boat comes in the early morning following a night of travel. It is surrounded by a barrier reef that forms magnificent turquoise lagoons and strips of sandy beaches. The high mountain is of volcanic origin and towers above the island at 235m. Not so long ago, they extracted semiprecious topaz stones here, including unique green stones. It is said that you can still find some here. This stone is also called «zabargad» by the Egyptians. You can still see traces of this activity on the island – a deserted mine, the remains of some structures, a cemetery and the road leading from the mine to a mooring area that is situated in a shallow bay off the east coast of the island.

The most popular place to dive is on the southern part of island. It is often called **Big Stone** or **Turtle Bay**. Usually this site is used as a night mooring and a base from which to investigate the next island - Rocky. However, this area should not be underestimated; it offers an excellent range of varied coral formations in rather shallow water, perfect for afternoon and evening dives full of surprises.

The reef wall goes down to 8-10m depth and passes into a sandy slope that runs along the south coast of the island. It is practically covered in coral turrets down to a depth of 30-35m. The turrets are made sculptural from hard corals and look like fantastic castles. This is a landscape full of breaks, hollows, labyrinths and gorges that form shelters for small reef fish, surrounded by a thick brushwood of soft and hard corals of a myriad colours.

Near to the port of Safaga, there is a popular dive site called «Tobia Arbaa» or «Seven Pillars». The first name is translated as «Four towers», the second one, «Seven towers». The second name is closer to reality as the turret-columns are generally five, but three of them are double. So it turns out about eight. Thus, we can name this southern site of Zabargad by the same token «Mie Tobia», or «Hundred pillars» («Hundred towers», or «Hundred columns») though, for sure no-one has counted how many there are! The quantity of these formations excels even the well-known site of Saint Johns «Umm El Arouk» («Mother of Ergs») also called «Woods», because of an abundance of turrets, columns and ergs.

The reef wall is also very beautiful with breaks, caves and swim-thorough, which can lead you through the reef to a lagoon. However there is no sense to swim away further where the visibility is lessened due to a sandy bottom and waves. Having reached the turquoise luminescence at the exit of a tunnel to a lagoon, it is far better to return back to the plateau.

In general the inhabitants of this site vary enormously, from tiny anthias up to huge groupers and giant moray eels. There are many large fish, which travel between the turrets, including stingrays, eagle rays and crocodile fish. One of the names of this site is «Turtle Bay». One can meet here a lot of friendly giant green turtles. Meetings with sharks, mantas, barracudas and tunas are also common. There are a lot of napoleons and groupers; also many invertebrates such as cuttlefish, squid, octopus and nudibranch, especially at night.

On the way back from the dive, the zodiac can pass above the reef and drop you on the island, where it's possible to wander on the beach, climb the top or examine the deserted mine. Zabargad is often underestimated compared to its neighbouring Rocky Island. This is sad as the former is a charming and magnificent site.

Location:
269 km on the southeast from Port Ghalib.
60 km on the south from a Daedalus reef

Co-ordinates (GPS - position):
23°35'57.11" N; 36°12'33.89" E
(Turtle Bay mooring)

Access:
Safari from Port Ghalib

Mooring:
South coast of the Island

Recommended level:
CMAS ** / PADI AOWD

Average depth:
16 m.

Maximum depth:
35 m. (at plateau edge)

Current:
Weak (less than 1 knots)

Visibility:
Good (20-25 m)

Type of dives:
- Reef
- Night

This is the biggest of the islands in this part of the sea and also forms part of the protected natural zone «Marine Park» of Egypt. There are a lot of places to dive that suit all tastes and levels. The shipwreck at the east coast is the biggest in this area at an accessible depth.

The huge coral garden at «Turtle Bay» is in an excellent condition. A fine place, and not only for night dives.

zabargad island

st. johns island, gezirat zabargad

Southeast Coast

On the east-south part of the island there are two great lagoons, which offer safe anchor mooring. The first great lagoon is **Jetty Lagoon** (the Lagoon of the Mooring). Here there is a mooring, the underwater part of its designs is covered by corals. Ashore it is possible to see the ruins of miner's constructions. This sandy lagoon is not so interesting. However, here there are a lot of good ergs, and it's often a spot to find reef sharks having a rest (lemon and nurse sharks). This quite a fine place for a night dive and further encounters with nudibranches, octopus and squid.

The second lagoon is situated to the south of the mooring and is called **Lagoon of the Doves**. It is less accessible by boat, but can be reached by swimming or zodiac. Here there are plenty of untouched coral slopes and plentiful shoals of fish. A variety of crustaceans and molluscs go onto the reef to eat here.

Khanka wreck

There is little information about the Russian transport ship named Khanka, built in 1969 and sunk in a southern bay at the east coast of Zabargad Island. The boat was 70m long and lies horizontally at a depth of 24m on the western part of a southern bay. Except for torn off head part lying on one side, on the part of port, it is practically not destroyed. The holds, bridge, an engine room and kitchen are easily accessible. The whole deck is well visible and the mast fixed by cables on both sides of the deck superstructure practically reaches the surface. The small coral colonies that grow on the hull show that the wreck has not been there for a long time.

Small glassfish fill the head section, which is not completely separated from the hull. A lot of pieces of electrical equipment are dispersed around the reef and directly around the hull. It seems likely that this was a reconnaissance boat. Though there is no real confirmation in support of this theory, it creates an interesting legend for this shipwreck. Visibility is changeable. The opened lifeboats (UK, pneumatic) lie on coast and on the other hand a bay. They are too big for places of saving tools' fastening on Khanka. They wrong point towards another shipwreck, Maidan, which really lies on the slopes of Rocky Island.

Neptuna wreck

On the western part of the island are the remains of a German safari boat which struck the reef. The boat had been altered from a mine trawler constructed in 1941 in Scotland. It apparently sank on April 29th 1981. The wreck is strongly broken apart and its remains are dispersed over the reef. Pipes, adjustments, bars and other boat parts litter the sea bottom.

External Walls

Outside of the lagoons are significant walls. Strong currents provide all the hallmarks of classic wall dives; here you can observe several types of sharks including Oceanic Grey, the Shark-fox, Silvertip and Tiger. There are also mantas and even whale sharks. Various soft and hard corals cover rocky breakages of ledges downwards to more than 30m. Visibility here is not so crystal as on Rocky Island (the reason is sand which is constantly blown off from the lagoons by the current).

Location:
269 km. on the southeast from Port Ghalib
60 km. on the south from a Daedalus reef and 5,5 km on the north from Rocky Island

Co-ordinates (GPS - position):
Jetty Lagoon:
23°37'06.96" N; 36°12'3.66" E
Khanka wreck:
23°36'55.40" N; 36°12'11.19" E
Neptuna wreck
23°36'21.91" N; 36°11'09.10" E

Access:
Safari from Port Ghalib

Mooring:
South and east coast of the Island

Recommended level:
CMAS ** / PADI AOWD

Average depth:
16 m.

Maximum depth:
More than 100 m.

Current:
Basically, except external walls, weak (less than 1 knot)

Visibility:
Good (20-25 m)

Type of dives:
- Reef
- Deep
- Wreck
- Wall
- Night

A big island with many varied and practically untouched dive sites for all levels and experience.

khanka wreck (zabargad island)
A. Shestopalets 2006

ras banas

mikauwa island

st. johns reef system

Habili Ali	41-42
Habili Gafar	43-44
Abu Bassala	45-46
Dangerous	47-48
Gota Kebir	49-50
Gota Sogayar	51-52
Caves	53-54
Mikauwa	55-56

umm khararim (caves)

zabargad island

rocky island

woods
gota sogayar
habili gafar
habili ali
abu bassala
gota kebir

dangerous

0   10   20 km.

Copyright © 2007 Andrei DVORETSKI www.r-divers.ru

habili ali

alternative names: abili ali, sha'ab ali

This is the nearest of the reefs of St. Johns on the way from the Zabargad Island. This reef grows from the depths and its top lies beneath the surface at 3-5m. The reef is oval and cone-shaped, and extends on an east-west axis. The slopes have no obvious plateaus but there is a small ledge-shelf on the southwest wall at 20-35m. This is a convenient lookout for sharks. As is usual on similar reefs, there are shoals of barracudas, jackfish and tunas. Here on the southern part, at the edge of a ledge at 40m, there is a large cleft in the body of the reef like a cave.

At a depth of 30-40m one can see magnificent gorgonians. The top part of the reef and especially its eastern part from 20m and above are covered with soft corals and marked with many caves and grottoes that give shelter to reef life including groupers and napoleons.

After staying for a while on the southwest ledge shark spotting, you then pass onto the northern part of the reef. Keeping it on your right, you can begin a gradual ascent along the wall moving southeast.

You will finish the dive at the mooring point on the southeast wall. The size of the reef allows for a full circle of the perimeter in one dive so long as the currents allow. The top of the reef at 3-5m can create certain difficulties as you near the surface. Just as you are ready to make your safety stop, you enter a zone of not just surface roughness, but also a descending current over the reef.

Reef shark. Habili Ali. A. Shestopalets 2006

Location:
Saint Johns reefs area 30 km on southwest from Zabargad Island. 130 km on southeast from Hamata

Co-ordinates (GPS - position):
23°25'5.28" N; 35°59'18.60" E

Access:
Safari from Hamata, Marsa Alam or Port Galib

Mooring:
South site of the reef

Recommended level:
CMAS ** / PADI AOWD

Average depth:
30 m.

Maximum depth:
More than 100 m.

Current:
Not strong (1-2 knots)

Visibility:
Good (20-35 m.)

Type of dives:
- Reef
- Drift
- Wall

This is the first of the reefs of this «habili» type on this route and is a little bit larger than normal. The walls offer many small ledges, clefts and even caves.

One can see fine coral colonies, including huge gorgonian and whip corals.

There is ample marine life including reef and oceanic sharks.

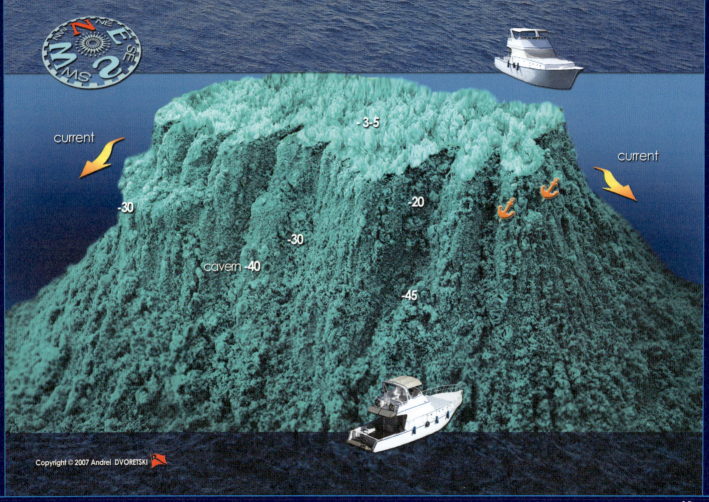

habili gafar

alternative names: abili gaffar, st. johns erg

This small oval and very nice reef is a component of the reef system St Johns. The top of the reef lies below the surface at 3-4m. Habili means "not grown» in Arabic and this name is typically given to reefs with this feature.

The reef is cone-shaped and its walls continue to great depths. The slopes of the cone are not flat but have a ledge at 20-35m round the entire perimeter. Shoals of barracuda, jack fish and tuna gather mainly on the northern part where the current can be very strong. This gives excellent opportunities to observe white tip and even grey reef sharks.

The top 15m of this reef are completely covered with soft pink-violet corals, offering homes to a thousand gold and violet anthias. In the ledges and cracks of the many hard corals colonies you can find lionfish and grouper. Around 20m the reef wall is considerably concave inside, forming a spacious cleft in which lionfish, butterfly fish and masked puffer hang out. Some big napoleons and parrot fish also prefer this place.

A dive on this reef represents a simple and gradual ascent along the walls of the cone following a spiral pattern, or if the current complicates matters, a rise by «shuttle» protected from the current. The reef is so small that it is easy to make one, two or even three turns around it during one dive.

Red octopus. Habili Gafar. A. Shestopalets 2006

Location:
40 km to west from Zabargad Island and 12 km to northwest from Habili Ali. 130 km to southeast from Hamata

Co-ordinates (GPS - position):
23°25'43.18" N; 35°52'36.46" E

Access:
Safari from Hamata, Marsa Alam or Port Galib

Mooring:
South site of the reef

Recommended level:
CMAS ** / PADI AOWD

Average depth:
30 m.

Maximum depth:
More than 100 m.

Current:
Not strong (1-2 knots)

Visibility:
Good (20-35 м)

Type of dives:
- Reef
- Drift
- Wall

One more «habili» on this route. It is much less in size, but equally rich with corals and living creatures than its relative «Ali».

The small size of the reef allows you to make some circles around it, rising upwards on a spiral. This does not give a sensation of repetition.

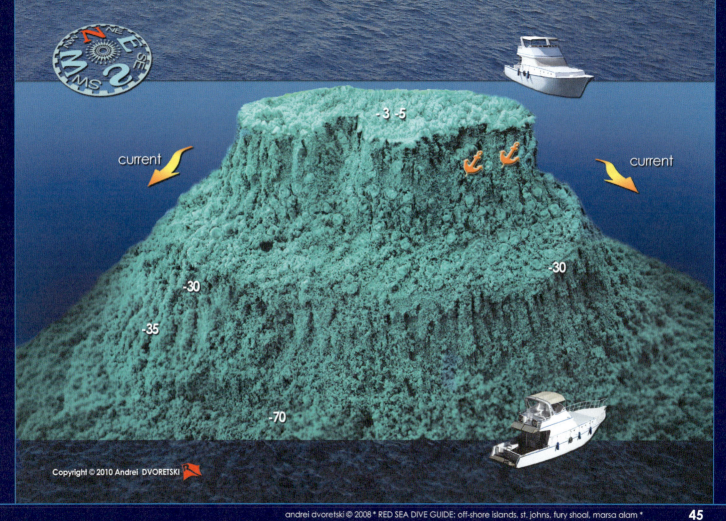

abu bassala

alternative names: sha'ab abu basala

The large sickle-shaped reef is one of the best places for spending the night. This reef is so big that it can offer three or four quite different dive plans. The main places for mooring are on the southern concave part of the reef, and the best are in a southeast and southwest position. From here it is possible to make an after-dinner dive by zodiac on the external reef wall, and also a fascinating night dive, entering the water from the boat and exploring the nearby reef wall, columns and ergs.

The whole external northern part of the reef is punctuated by cracks, ledges, folds and deep grottoes cutting into the walls. Close to the northeast corner, the reef is particularly broken up into separate columns and ergs. The bottom of the reef lies around 15-18m and the current affords excellent visibility and extensive coral formations. The current can complicate moving forward but the broken reef and turrets break it down. At the corner of the reef, the current gradually weakens and practically disappears on the internal part. Here it is possible to look around for an ideal night dive spot.

The western part of the reef is also ideal if the currents are prohibitive and is much better lit in the afternoon. Here the current drifts by and the reef is equally beautiful. The dive ends in the current-free area of the internal part of the reef, again, an ideal spot for night diving amongst the columns, turrets and ergs.

Location:
Saint Johns reefs area
40 km. to west from Zabargad
12 km to west from Habili Ali

Co-ordinates (GPS - position):
23°23'16.62" N; 35°48'38.12" E

Access:
Safari from Hamata, Marsa Alam or Port Galib

Mooring:
South of the reef

Recommended level:
CMAS* / PADI OWD

Average depth:
14 m.

Maximum depth:
25 m.

Current:
Weak (less than 1 knot)

Visibility:
Good (20-25 m)

Type of dives:
- Reef
- Drift
- Night

Well-sheltered places on the south guarantee quiet mooring and a reef with many picturesque places for relaxing dives and night dives.

The west and southeast extremities of the main reef have been cut up by canyons, grottoes and caves, and also many coral turrets and columns, which are especially attractive.

Blackspotted sweetlips. Abu Bassala. A. Shestopalets 2006

dangerous

dangerous reef, reef dangloss

Location:
47 km to southwest from Zabargad Island. 17 km on southwest from Habili Ali

Co-ordinates (GPS - position):
23°20'23.22" N; 35°51'16.26" E

Access:
Safari from Hamata, Marsa Alam or Port Galib

Mooring:
South site of the reef

Recommended level:
CMAS* / PADI OWD

Average depth:
14 m.

Maximum depth:
25 m.

Current:
Weak (less than 1 knot)

Visibility:
Good (20-25 m)

Type of dives:
- Reef
- Cavern
- Night

Dangerous Reef is the most southerly of the St Johns reefs. Despite the name, this mid-size reef offers a quiet and not too deep resting place for an overnight mooring and for evening and night dives. The southwest extremity of the reef is rounded and gives an unusual mooring place. The wall of hard corals goes down to around 22m where it leads into a flat sandy bottom with small coral bushes, columns and ergs around which swim napoleons and moray eels.

The internal, southern part of the reef wall has a lot of cracks and breaks around 8m depth that form swim-through from 4-10m with sandy bottoms. Often closed from above, the entrance and exit routes of these small grottoes and tunnels are always visible, making them safe for penetration. Blue spotted stingrays appear on the sandy bottoms and large groupers peer out from the clefts. In some passages, a weak current attracts small white tip reef sharks resting before night hunting. At the entrance to the tunnels, huge anemones shelter big families of anemone fish.

On the east and on the west side there are fine coral gardens where great stone corals cascade downwards from the reef. Amongst these corals live many small fish - sergeants, a flute, butterfly fish and a lot of different Red Sea groupers.

This reef is well protected and offers a fine location for a night dive. As usual, a small current is possible coming from the north. It is almost absent at the reef wall but may be felt at the southern edge of the coral gardens. If, having passed along the reef wall in a western direction, you will turn to the south at the coral garden and find the current here to take you back to the boat. At night on the reef you will meet cuttlefish and octopus, small reef sharks hunting, free swimming morays, and even the occasional Spanish Dancer.

Red sea anemonefish. Dangerous reef. A. Shestopalets 2006

Contrary to the name, this reef is so calm, quiet and safe that it is very often used as a place for night mooring.

The southwest extremity of the reef is cut by clefts, tunnels and grottoes that are easily accessible. The reef is also attractive for daytime dives amongst the many picturesque reef pyramids and columns.

gota kebir

alternative names: big gota, gota kibeer

Location: 120 km on south from Hamata 19 km on east from Abu Bassala

Co-ordinates (GPS - position): 23°25'11.58" N; 35°56'33.04" E

Access: Safari from Hamata, Marsa Alam or Port Galib

Mooring: South site of the reef

Recommended level: CMAS** / PADI AOWD

Average depth: 30 m.

Maximum depth: More than 100 m.

Current: Strong (more than 2 knots)

Visibility: Good (25-35 m)

Type of dives:
- Reef
- Deep
- Drift

Gota Kebir in translation from Arabic means «the biggest part» and this reef is large and oval in shape. Its size means a number of different dives are possible depending on the weather and the current (usually from north to south). The northern part has two plateaus at 15m and 35m, which are perfect for watching white tip and grey sharks that swim along the edge of the reef. Here you can also find blue spotted stingrays.

As you dive along the steep east wall above the plateau heading south, you can look out into the blue to spot pelagics cruising by. The last 15m of the reef are no so heavily populated with soft corals as some other reefs in St Johns (such as Habili Gafar or Gota Sogayar). However, there is a large gorgonian at 30m and many red corals. The top 10m of the reef is ideal for meeting turtles, as is the southeast corner where the surface of the wall has great ledges, and deeper cracks that even form grottoes and caves. Penetration is possible in some places. The area where you finish the dive has some large groups of anemones around 8-10m that are just perfect for photo opportunities.

Typical of most reefs called «Gota», this reef pyramid offers vigorous diving with a current that runs along plunging steep walls covered by hard corals.

Here there are many chances to meet oceanic and reef sharks and other large predators.

White-tip reef shark. A. Shestopalets 2006.

gota sogayar

alternative names: small gota, gota sagir

Gota Sogayar in translation from Arabic means «the small part». The walls of this small oval-shaped reef fall steeply into the abyss around the entire perimeter. The top few metres are covered entirely by colourful soft corals and abound with various tiny sea life. Small shoals of tuna and young barracuda turn around searching for any opportunity to eat. Long pink and red coral whips extend into the blue. At 20-30 m there are magnificent gorgonians. Shoals of mackerel and jackfish swim in the distance. A whole family of humphead parrots and napoleons majestically float around the perimeter of the reef.

The current is usually running from north to south here. Therefore, it's best to begin the dive from the northern extremity of the reef and drift with the current back to the boat, which has moored in the southern part. The south has a series of grottoes, cracks and clefts in the reef, which are perfect to explore whilst enjoying your safety stop.

Location: Saint Johns reefs area
123 km to south from Hamata
4 km to northwest from Gota Kebir

Co-ordinates (GPS - position): 23°25'49.94" N; 35°54'16.03" E

Access: Safari from Hamata, Marsa Alam or Port Galib

Mooring: Южная оконечность рифа

Recommended level: CMAS** / PADI AOWD

Average depth: 30 m.

Maximum depth: More than 100 m.

Current: Strong (more than 2 knots)

Visibility: Good (25-35 m)

Type of dives:
- Reef
- Drift
- Deep

Yet another «Gota», this time a little bit smaller, but still worthy of the name.

This reef has everything you need for wall diving – steep coral-covered reef walls, currents and depth.

As with similar sites, here there are plenty of opportunities to meet oceanic and reef sharks and other large predators.

Grouper. Gota Sogayar. A. Shestopalets 2006

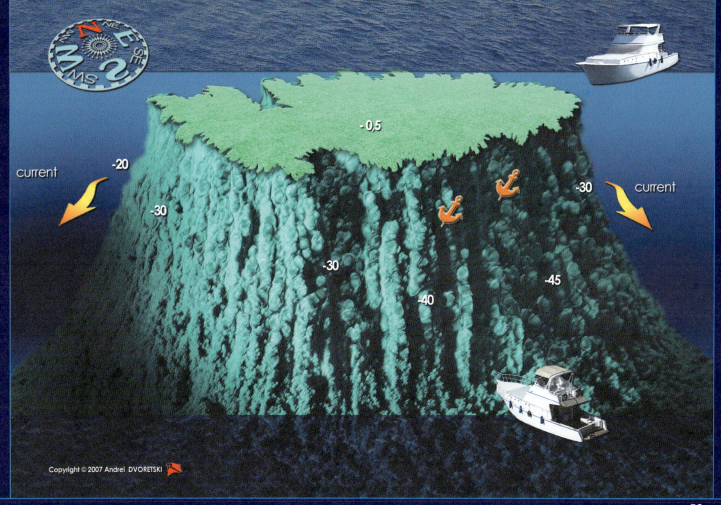

caves

alternative names: umm khararim

This is the most interesting «cave» reef in this part of the sea. It is generally considered to be located outside of the St Johns reef system and in any case, it is the furthest north. As a rule, this site is usually kept for two dives as the boat moves north to moor overnight at the island of Mikawa.

The main part of the reef forms a letter "L" with a myriad of smaller reef parts and ergs around. Practically the whole body of the reef is cut through with cracks and tunnels. The main part of these is open from above making them well lit. If you lose your bearings on the dive it is possible to surface in one of these «windows» in the arches and to look round to find an exit from the labyrinth. There is no need to carry a torch during the day, although it can be useful to see the true colours of the corals and for peeking into secluded corners and cracks. The boat usually moors in the southern part of the reef, close to the eastern edge. The depth here is around 20-25m and the area is home to several large napoleons.

In a northerly direction from the boat where the moorings are tied, there are two entrances in the reef wall, leading into a system of tunnels. The best way to dive is to move in a western direction (with your right shoulder to the reef) ignoring these two entrances. In 2-3 minutes you will find a single entrance. Enter the labyrinth here. The twisting corridor (to the left, to the right, then again to the left) will lead you to a nice «hall», fenced from the north and north-east by a very nice colony of hard coral boulders, up to a depth of about 5-6m. It is possible to pass through this «barrier» to the outside. The whole eastern part of the reef is a rich coral garden, which forms a wall of the reef and comes to an end at its bottom at about 15-18m as white coral sand.

If you enjoyed the «cave», then when you pass the «hall» on the perimeter and are just about to return to your entry point, turn a little bit to the right and head west to swim through some fascinating labyrinthine passages. There are several twists and turns but the whole area is well lit. You may get a surprise in the form of a small reef shark or stingray dozing in the sand. Watch out for a slight current, which can make swimming difficult, and be careful not to stir up the bottom with too much finning. Try to not touch the walls as they are home to many scorpion fish. Catch the «pulse» of this current and continue moving forward. Try not to go too far into the passages leading to the north as many are dead-ends and impassable cracks. If you head in the right direction (west-northwest) you will reach the exit to the external western wall of the reef. The exit is beautifully lit in the blue and a small northerly current guarantees fine visibility. Near to the exit there is a very picturesque turret covered by soft corals, surrounded by bright small fishes. Keeping the reef at your left shoulder, keep moving first south and then east along the reef wall, around the turrets and ergs before coming back to the boat. On the way you will meet morays, stingrays and a napoleon waiting at the end for you. In the spring (March-April), there is a good chance to see mantas at the surface here.

In general there are a lot of varied dives on this reef. The best will be the one that you choose independently because here it is better to dive in small groups or pairs. Without a doubt you should make a second dive here - it will be different and far more interesting than the first one, even if you try to repeat it.

Location:
97,5 km to south from Hamata
23 km to north from Gota Sogayar

Co-ordinates (GPS - position):
23°37'33.02" N; 35°49'34.59" E

Access:
Safari from Hamata, Marsa Alam or Port Galib

Mooring:
South and southeast side

Recommended level:
CMAS* / PADI OWD

Average depth:
12 m.

Maximum depth:
20 m.

Current:
Weak (less than 1 knot)

Visibility:
Good (20-25 m)

Type of dives:
 - Reef
 - Cavern
 - Cave

The most northern of the reefs in this group, this reef is more like an independent group in itself formed from two great reef blocks. One of these is known as «Caves», and the second is called «Paradise» and lies some half kilometre to the west, surrounded by several smaller reefs and ergs.

mikauwa island

sirnaka island
geziret syrnaka

Location:
71 km to south from Hamata
23 km to north from Caves

Co-ordinates (GPS - position):
23°49'49.39" N; 35°48'41.18" E

Access:
Safari from Hamata, Marsa Alam or Port Galib

Mooring:
South coast of Island

Recommended level:
CMAS* / PADI OWD

Average depth:
14 m.

Maximum depth:
25 m.

Current:
Weak (less than 1 knot)

Visibility:
Good (20-25 m)

Type of dives:
- Reef
- Wreck
- Night

This island is the end point of travel to St Johns, and the usual overnight mooring place prior to the transition to Fury Shoal.

The low island offers protection from the strong northern winds rough seas. The boat moors at the southern edge of the island, close to the eastern point. An interesting barrier reef surrounds its rocky coast. The body of the reef is penetrated with clefts and passages, and the bottom of the reef is surrounded with many turrets, columns and erg-habili, which are covered in soft corals and do not touch the surface. The base of the reef is about 10-12m, before it continues as a hollow south to a depth of 30m, before breaking up at 55m and falling into the deep. The area between the mooring and the barrier reef is a fine place for a night dive with an average depth of 15m. It is packed with various marine life: small fry, large groupers, huge morays and slopes. There are a lot of nudibranches, molluscs and squid. There are octopus and sometimes you can spot reef sharks going out for night hunting.

If you are visiting the island during the day, the sunken fishing trawler will be of some interest. The boat may be small but it is covered in corals and living creatures. It lies on a steep slope and has moved deeper over time from 30m to the stern now resting on 55m. The hull, steering cabin, superstructures, masts and an engine room are very well kept. The boat lies to the west of the lighthouse at a distance of approximately 70m and slightly to the south. A good reference point for finding is a large part of a net, caught on a fragment of coral formation on the crest of a precipice about 27m, which has kept the trawler from further slipping to an inaccessible depth. The boat can be seen from around 10m but poor visibility and strong currents can make both the dive, and finding the boat, difficult. This is a great spot for dramatic photography.

This low coral island is perfectly situated to offer shelter from the northern wind, giving excellent overnight mooring. The reef surrounding the island is home to a lot of marine creatures and makes an excellent choice for a night dive.

If you come here during the day, it's possible to make a dive on the wreck of a fishing trawler, which has come to rest on the edge of a wide plateau near to a lighthouse.

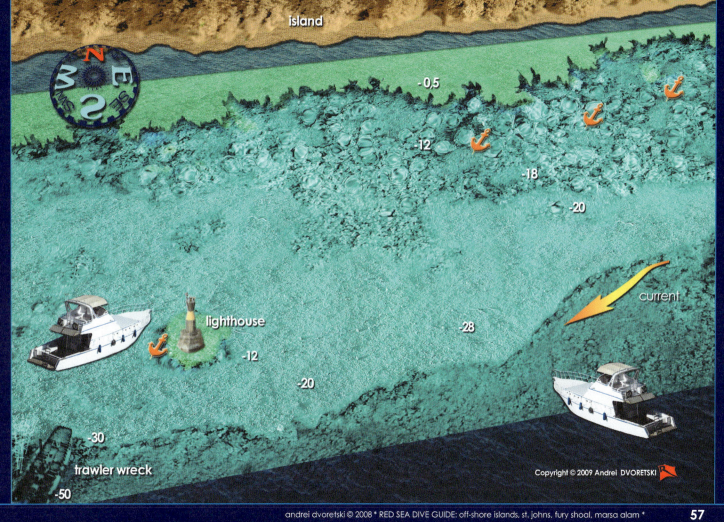

big red octopus
A. Shestopelets 2006

sha'ab maksour

sha'ab maksour, mansur reef

This large reef is around 500m long and extends from north to south with a slight bend. There is a plateau at the northern and southern ends of the reef between 15-40m. Maksour in translation from Arabic means «broken» and it completely corresponds to the underwater relief: breaks, abysses and tunnels. One of the most beautiful places is the southern plateau with its underwater hills and turrets. The biggest of them is located at an entrance to a tunnel at 15m, quite safe for penetration and leading to a cave 40m deep. There are several arch exits to the external reef wall, lit with bright blue light at 40, 46 and 55m.

This type of dive is not recommended for those without some experience (that of cavern dives on reefs like Sha'ab Claudio is not really sufficient). The boat moors above the south plateau where it is possible to make two dives. You can also dive the east wall as a drift from a zodiac, passing to the plateau with the northerly current. One can see hard corals, gorgonian fans and knotted fan corals. Sharks are common here. In the blue are shoals of tuna and young barracuda with more adult barracuda above you. As you cross to the plateau the depth is around 15m. As you complete your dive, there are plenty of opportunities to enjoy swimming around the turrets and columns, accompanied by reef fish, great emperors, napoleon, parrot fish and groupers who watch from their shelters.

The second type of dive here is from a boat or RIB right on the plateau. If the dive is later in the morning, you might see sharks at the edge of the plateau out in the blue. Take a relaxed pace around the plateau and the three big hills that lie to the north. Here the plateau comes to an end at the reef at a depth of 12-15m and the columns and turrets as described above. There is a light current here.

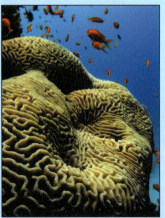

The northern plateau is also interesting and more complex to dive as the split point of the current breaks here into two streams that bend around the plateau and then the reef. At the corners, contrary currents cause some turbulence. These whimsical currents make for an «ironing» dive.

It is best to start the dive from a zodiac at the northeast edge of the plateau and head at your maximum depth to the Northern Cape. Here on the wall there are magnificent bushes of gorgonians and branches of whip corals and, of course, the possibility to observe sharks, tuna and barracuda is high. There is a plethora of soft corals, sponges, gorgonians and fan corals. Look out for white tip sharks and marlin. Then you turn to the south and cover a wide zigzag to return to the beginning of the plateau at a depth of 12-15m. The bottom cascades down with hard corals and soft coral formations. Groupers and morays guard the area and there is plentiful marine life. You can end the dive and re-join the zodiac at the western corner of the reef as far as possible to the south. Here the reef is a little concave and better protected than the northeast part. Even with a strong northerly wind, this is the preferred exit route for safety.

Location:
29 km. to east from Hamata
50 km. to north from Miauwa

Co-ordinates (GPS - position):
24°14'22.68" N; 35°39'9.36" E

Access:
Safari from Hamata, Marsa Alam and Port Ghalib

Mooring:
All south site of the reef

Recommended level:
CMAS** / PADI AOWD

Average depth:
30 m.

Maximum depth:
More than 100 m.

Current:
Strong (more than 2 knots)

Visibility:
Good (25-30 m)

Type of dives:
- Reef
- Drift
- Deep

This is the first reef in the dive program of the Fury Shoal reef system.

It is a big reef with two magnificent plateaus at the northern and southern ends. A rather large cave on the south plateau, deeper than 40m, exits to the external wall. This reef offers fine visibility, excellent corals and a lot of different reef creatures. There is also a high chance to see sharks and dolphins.

sha'ab claudia

alternative names:
sha'ab cloude

Location:
25 км. to east from Hamata
4,5 км. to west from Sha'ab Maksour

Co-ordinates (GPS - position):
24°13'13.50" N; 35°36'44.82" E

Access:
Safari from Hamata, Marsa Alam and Port Ghalib

Mooring:
All south site of the reef

Recommended level:
CMAS* / PADI OWD

Average depth:
12 m.

Maximum depth:
20 m.

Current:
Weak (less than 1 knot)

Visibility:
Good (20-25 m)

Type of dives:
- Reef
- Cavern
- Caves

This is a cave-like reef similar to the "Caves" in St Johns but with a simpler labyrinth and more comfortable passages and swim-thorough.

This small oval-shaped reef is almost entirely cut through in the northwest with picturesque passages. Once inside, the light and shadow play on the walls is very impressive. A small current practically guarantees good visibility, especially when diving in pairs with some interval between each pair.

Moorings are typically undertaken on the south and southwest edge of the reef. It is possible to dive directly from the boat and the depth is 18m with no current. The whole perimeter of the reef is surrounded with magnificent dome-shaped cone corals. Keeping these to your right, you head north to a turret where you will likely feel a light counter-current. It is easily overcome before heading further north to the passages through to the east part if the reef and two adjoining turrets which extend along the wall. Here, reef sharks doze away the day waiting for their night hunting. Essentially completing the circle takes you back to where you started, albeit with the reef wall a little closer, and above the domes. If you have enough air (100 bar or more) you can make a small excursion into the labyrinth where there are two entrances at 8m. Moving through the passages in a north-northwest direction leads you to the external northern wall. By keeping the reef to your left shoulder you can return to your exit place. Look out for morays, stingrays and napoleon fish.

This place is perfect for a relaxing buddy team dive and offers the ideal chance to practice buoyancy control. This reef is also perfect for photo and video opportunities - the twilight of the cave contrasting deeply with the up-lighting in the tunnels of the labyrinth.

Inside a cave. Sha'ab Claudia. A. Shestopalets 2006

One of the most unusual reefs in this part of the sea. The hard corals are in an excellent condition and almost surround the entire reef. The best variant for dives - pair, or small groups, a maximum on 4-6 persons.
The tunnels and passages in the southwest are very exciting. Two dives here are never the same.

el malahi

sha'ab el malahi, malahi park

This is a small reef, as if formed from densely packed ergs, which form an underwater labyrinth of corridors, tunnels and passages. It is last cave-like reef on this route and is situated around 5km from **Sha'ab Claudia**. You can choose which one of these dives to make first based on the number of boats there.

El Malahi means "children's playground" when translated from the Arabic and this more than sums up a dive in this remarkably beautiful place. It is very relaxing here – shallow depths, little or no current between the ergs and plenty of time to chill out. There is also excellent visibility here. A special atmosphere is created from the solar rays dancing in the darkened spaces of these underwater galleries. As you look out from the caves, the bright blue light is particularly beautiful, highlighting all the individual sponges and interior features.

The reef is very rich with living creatures and coral in mint condition. Napoleons grandly pass near to the moorings. Buried in the sand in the many passageways, cracks and clefts, are morays, groupers and octopus waiting to trap their prey. It is quite common here to see a pod of dolphins. As with all «cave» reefs, it's best to dive this site in small groups and pairs.

Location:
30,5 km to southeast from Hamata. 5,5 km. to southwest from Claudia

Co-ordinates (GPS - position):
24°11'45.30" N; 35°39'34.86" E

Access:
Safari from Hamata, Marsa Alam and Port Ghalib

Mooring:
All south site of the reef

Recommended level:
CMAS* / PADI OWD

Average depth:
12 m.

Maximum depth:
20 m.

Current:
Weak (less than 1 knot)

Visibility:
Good (20-25 m)

Type of dives:
- Reef
- Caves
- Cavern

An absolutely fantastic reef and a close relative of Sha'ab Claudia, both in terms of structure and situation. However, the passes and canyons of this labyrinth are more open and somewhat quieter. It is like an amalgam of many tiny reefs formed together. Claudia and Malahi are two reefs that cannot be missed on any southern safari itinerary. To miss a dive on either of them is simply inexcusable!

Arabian cardinalfish. A. Shestopalets 2006

abu galava

abu galava kebir
abu galava sogayar

Sha'ab Abu Galawa Kebir is one of the most northerly reefs of the group Fury Shoal. This large reef is around 500m long by 100m wide and is concave in the south. The northern part of the reef offers four internal closed lagoons. Galawa means turquoise-blue colour in Arabic, and the reef is thus named due to the fantastic shades of the lagoons.

The western wall of the reef forms ledges, openings and canyons along its whole length. About 100m southwest from the western end of the main reef there are many large ergs. The first of these ergs has the wreck of a sunken towboat, the Tien Hsing (Tienstin). Constructed in Shanghai in 1935, the boat was travelling from Suez to the south when it struck the reef and sank in October 1943. The length of the boat is approximately 35m. Its head part is grown into the reef wall at the surface. The hull is a little bit inclined to the right lying along the reef and to the stern, which rests on the bottom at 17 m. The head of the boat touches the surface. It is best to dive here from a zodiac having passed some distance along the reef. It is also possible to dive from the mooring at the southern part of the western end of the reef and swim in a south-westerly direction to reach here. The bottom is flat and lies around 16-17m but the current can be quite strong. The hull is covered by soft and hard corals and is home to many creatures. The side barrier has moved into the sand. Two doorways on right side provide easy access to the top cabin and to the metal ladder leading to an engine room. The third doorway from the right leads to a toilet with the toilet bowl still intact. Near to the head part, there is a cleft and small grotto-like cave in the reef. It's possible to swim here for a while, admiring the game of light and shadow.

If the current allows, this is an excellent place for a night dive. The well-protected western extremity of the main reef boasts plentiful marine life including morays, lionfish, sleeping parrotfish and Spanish dancers.

Sha'ab Abu Galawa Sogayar is the second reef in this group. It is quite shallow and well protected from the northern wind and currents. It is common to make a check dive here for safaris leaving from Hamata or Marsa Alam; alternatively an evening or night dive on the way back from St Johns.

At the western end of the reef as it follows around from the north, you can enter a canyon at around 15m. As you move on, it appears that you are reaching a dead-end, but if you move towards the surface to 5m, it is possible to pass through a V-shaped passage to a sandy lagoon in the centre of the reef. The passage ends at around 8m and fantastic colonies of corals cascade down. The table corals are so big here it is like swimming under the branches of a Christmas tree. There are two exits from the sandy lagoon that lead to the eastern reef. Keeping the reef to your right shoulder will lead you back to the boat.

On the southwest, at the bottom of the reef lies the shipwreck Endimon. It belonged to an Australian, Anthony Corbin, and now lies at 18m on a sandy bottom. At just 16m length, this small boat is filled with glassfish and very pretty. It is practically undamaged, although it has already lost its furniture, superstructures and the main mast.

The hull of the boat is actively colonized by soft and hard corals and gives habitation and food to a lot of fish. The stainless steel of the main mast fastening still shines on the remaining construction of the deck and many other details are still intact and in a good condition.

Location:
21 km to southeast for Hamata
4 km from Sha'ab Claudia

Co-ordinates (GPS - position):
Abu Galava Kebir:
24°13'41.52" N; 35°34'25.80" E
Abu Galava Sogayar:
24°15'3.72" N; 35°32'26.16" E

Access:
Safari from Hamata, Marsa Alam and Port Ghalib

Mooring:
Southwest site

Recommended level:
CMAS* / PADI OWD

Average depth:
12 m.

Maximum depth:
20 m.

Current:
Weak (less than 1 knot)

Visibility:
Good (20-25 m)

Type of dives:
- Reef
- Wreck
- Night

This reef is well protected from the waves and is used as an overnight mooring place for boats returning from St Johns and as «training» for safaris starting from Hamata.
There are two shipwrecks here, one on each reef, which are perfect for night dives.

sha'ab sharm

alternative names: gota sharm

The prevailing winds in this region are northern and can make for rough journeys when travelling back from the distant south. In order to minimise inconvenience to passengers and the chance of seasickness, the whole distance from Fury Shoal to Marsa Alam is often broken into smaller parts. This can impact on the time spent in either St Johns or Fury Shoal as visits to less remote reefs are included on the trip north. Very often it's preferred to miss a day or so at St Johns in favour of more dives at Elphinstoun.

The reefs between north and south are also very interesting and deserve to be dived. Sha'ab Sharm is often the location for one or even two days diving, and Sha'ab Marsa Alam, some 35km north, is ideal for evening and night dives. Leaving early in the morning from Sha'ab Marsa Alam, your boat can quickly reach Elphinstoun, 32km to the north.

Sha'ab Sharm is a big reef, 450m in length that stands alone in the sea. Its oval shape extends from east to west. In terms of location, size and type, this reef is similar to Little Brother, Gota Kebir or Sha'ab Ali, and it is equally rich with marine life. Tuna, mackerel and barracuda are commonplace here, as are many different kinds of sharks.

The northern and southern parts of the reef are steep walls that plunge to between 50-75m before flattening out. Colonies of soft and hard corals cover the walls and the current gives great visibility. On the west, the abrupt slope interrupts the rather narrow step surrounding the extremity of the reef at 18-20m. On the eastern edge of the reef there is a large plateau at 15-30m. The strong current comes from the north and splits into two at the northwest extremity of the reef, before proceeding along the external northern wall towards the east. There is little or no current on the internal southern wall.

The large size of the reef allows for at least two dives here. The first one should begin at the western plateau where you can look out for sharks before continuing on the outside northern wall, drifting along to the eastern point of the reef. If the current is strong enough it is sometimes possible to reach the eastern plateau where the waters are calm. If you have to surface before this, be sure to move away from the wall to avoid being thrown onto it by the surface current.

On the northwest extremity of the reef, the current divides into two, often strong, counter-currents that can make such a dive impossible. In this case, the dive is planned in another direction, along the plateau-step in the south, and further, along a southern wall on the east, back to the mooring. Here is no less picturesque than the north, and the quieter dive will allow you to observe more closely the coral wall with clefts and grottoes that shelter numerous creatures.

The second dive can be start at the southern edge of the east plateau at your maximum planned depth. Come to the edge of the plateau, holding it to your left side. Here, on the right, you again can see sharks. Then, at the vertical cleft, which edges the plateau in the north, you can ascent to the mooring along the reef. There is plenty of reef small fry here and on the left side some fine soft and hard corals. Look out for the large barracuda and napoleon as you end the dive.

Location:
11,5 km from the coastline
45 km to south from Marsa Alam

Co-ordinates (GPS - position):
West plateau:
24°47'14.29" N; 35°10'37.95" E
East plateau:
24°47'11.64" N; 35°10'54.32" E

Access:
Safari from Hamata, Marsa Alam and Port Ghalib

Mooring:
South and southeast extremities of the reef

Recommended level:
CMAS** / PADI AOWD

Average depth:
25 m.

Maximum depth:
More than 100 m.

Current:
Strong (more than 2 knots outside, on the north site of the reef)

Visibility:
Good (25-30 m)

Type of dives:
- Reef
- Wall
- Deep

A reef with remarkable walls and two plateaus on its extremities. The location of this reef is different to others here as it extends from northwest to east and therefore offers unusual conditions for this type of dive.

elphinstoun

elphinestone, elfine stoun, sha'ab shagra

Elphinstoun is a large isolated reef around 350m long and 70m wide that extends from southeast to northwest. There is a plateau at each end at least 100-150m wide at 25-40m depth. The walls of the central section of the reef drop away steeply to more than 100m. The current is usually strong and comes from the southeast but is changeable forming local currents. Dives here are complex and fascinating. The beauty of the underwater landscape and the wealth of marine life make Elphinstoun one of the best sites for wall diving in Egypt.

The northern plateau is the underwater continuation of the reef that peaks the surface. After about 50m, it falls to a depth of 4-6m, then is stepped to 18-20m, before smoothly continuing down over about 70m to a depth of 20-39m. The plateau gradually narrows and is also interrupted by a deep (55-58m) canyon. The plateau finally bottoms out around 70-75m. The current is from the north on the south and crosses the plateau sharply at its corner. Therefore it is best to start the dive somewhere in the mid-part, a little to the north of the edge, giving the time to pass to the main reef for your ascent. It is common to see sharks here. Above the surface of the plateau, look out for shoals of blue triggerfish and tuna and jackfish in pairs. Several huge barracuda stalk here. As you swim around the reef wall, keeping it on your right shoulder, you can drift with the current as you gradually ascend this magnificent wall.

The reef offers huge gorgonian and switch corals. Bushes of soft corals and colonies of hard corals cover its entirety. The clefts and grottoes of the wall hide morays and groupers. You will be accompanied by flutes, shoals of jackfish and mackerel. Angels, emperor fish, lionfish and never-ending anthias paint bright colours all over the beautiful coral-covered wall. Be sure to look out into the blue on your left side to try and spot oceanic white tips (Longimanus). They often pass by here with their eternal companions, the striped pilot fish.

Location:
25 km to north from Marsa Alam
35 km to south from Port Ghalib

Co-ordinates (GPS - position):
North plateau:
25°18'38.22" N; 34°51'47.18" E
South plateau:
25°18'25.57" N; 34°51'48.96" E

Access:
Safari from Hamata, Marsa Alam, Port Ghalib, dailyboats

Mooring:
South extremity

Recommended level:
CMAS** / PADI AOWD

Average depth:
30 m.

Maximum depth:
75 m.

Current:
Strong (more than 2 knots on the north plateau and on the walls)

Visibility:
Good (25-35 m)

Type of dives:
- Reef
- Wall
- Deep

A cult place, which makes a wonderful finale to your trip. Interestingly, it is not part of any nature protection national parks. And I think that it only an temporary mistake of the official responsible for it.

elphinstoun

elphinestone, elfine stoun, sha'ab shagra

At its southern tip, the main reef breaks close to the moorings and at a depth of 20 m passes into the southern plateau. This triangular «tongue» follows the oval form of the reef at 35m extending to 75m in width. At around 37-39, the plateau falls sharply to a depth of 70m where it eventually flattens out.

The **southern plateau** is extremely beautiful and covered by a garden of soft corals that are perfectly illuminated in the afternoon. There are many reef fish and pelagic predators. Sharks can be found left and right. The Longimanus often surprise divers near to the moorings as they return from their dives. They seem to enjoy teasing the divers with simulated attacks and causing excitement.

Right at the end of the plateau, about 60m to the south from the reef wall, there is the so-called «**Sarcophagus Arch**» - a swim-through, approximately 15 m long and 6 m wide. The vault of the arch sits around 50 m and the bottom at 65m. Close to the northern wall of the arch, a large rock lies at the bottom and resembles a sarcophagus or some say, an open book. The current through the arch is usually contrary and means that much air is expended to pass through. This dive is only recommended for skilled technical divers.

The **east wall** is spectacularly studded with huge gorgonian and soft corals. The only damage is near to the moorings in the south. This makes a magnificent drift dive from the middle of the reef, either south or north, depending on the current. The ledges of the coral shelter funny masked puffer fish, grottoes with moray eels inside, groupers and even white tip reef sharks. Look closely and do not forget to glance out into the blue for more shark sightings and even mantas. Either way, you are guaranteed to be accompanied by flutes, mackerel and barracudas. Owing to the currents here, the visibility is usually excellent.

The **western wall** is less steep and a little less stunning than the east. However, there are huge gorgonians and both soft and hard coral growth. There are a lot of ledges, grottoes and small caves occupied by titanic triggerfish and others like squirrel, groupers and morays. It is possible to begin the dive from the zodiac, from the visible end of the northern tip of the reef, moving south along the wall (with the reef to your left), and back to the mooring. As a variant, when there is weak or no current, you can dive directly from the boat at the corner of the southern plateau. First you move gradually shallower to the north (with the reef wall on your right), then turn around at 100 bar to head back to the south (the reef is now on your left side) and the mooring. You can finish your safety stop at 5m, swimming at the southern tip of the reef, protected from the currents, and in the company of huge napoleon fish, and even Longimanus sharks. The latter is incredibly rare, even in celebrated shark destinations such as South Africa. The Longimanus is indeed one of the gifts of the Red Sea and in particular, Elphinstoun. This is a particularly special place to dive as it represents the end of the safari. At best, there is just one shallower dive to go on one of the Abu Dabbab reefs and then it's back to Port Ghalib before sunset…

Location:
25 km Marsa Alam
35 km Port Ghalib

Co-ordinates (GPS - position):
North plateau:
25°18'38.22" N; 34°51'47.18" E
South plateau:
25°18'25.57" N; 34°51'48.96" E

Access:
Safari from Hamata, Marsa Alam, Port Ghalib, dailyboats

Mooring:
South extremity

Recommended level:
CMAS** / PADI AOWD

Average depth:
30 m.

Maximum depth:
75 m.

Current:
Strong (more than 2 knots on the north plateau and on the walls)

Visibility:
Good (25-35 m)

Type of dives:
- Reef
- Wall
- Deep

This reef is named in honour of Baron Elphinstoun Georges Keith (1746-1823), an English admiral who was successfully in charge of the fleet during wars in the Atlantic Ocean, in the Northern, Baltic and Mediterranean Seas and the Indian Ocean.
In 1815 he led the sending of Napoleon to Saint Helena Island.

abu dabbab

This is a group of six shallow reefs that generally sit around 15m and up to 25m in their external areas. It is impossible to dive them all, even over one day. It is most common to dive **Abu Dabbab 2 and 3** as they are most protected from the waves. Here at 15m you can see the remains of the boat Heaven One which sank in 2004 after a fire. Despite the fire damage, much of the wreck remains and is worth a dive. The engines are intact and the forward part contains many visible objects such as fans, lamps, electronic equipment, kitchen furniture and so on. Much of the construction remains in place and here you can spot a large coral grouper hiding from the current under the keel.

The reefs are very colourful and rich with marine life. There are stingrays, jackfish, tuna, barracudas, napoleon fish and small shoals of dolphins.

The big coral garden to the northeast of the main reef can be seen over a short time at the end of your dive. In this case, head east and you will soon encounter a barrier of coral formations. Between the northern wall of the reef and the main gardens mass, there is something like a passage at around 7m. Keeping the main reef at your right shoulder, soon you will come to another garden, which begins practically at the reef and extends in a southeast direction. The depth of the garden gradually increases as the stock of your air decreases. Therefore, we turn to the south-southwest, coming back to the southern wall of the reef, protected from the current. Lovely coral formations and reef creatures make your ascent to the mooring a pleasant one.

This garden is worth a separate dive too. You should begin near to the middle of the external part of the reef, close to the east. An ideal entry point into the water is a turret, which joins the main reef at about 10m depth. Keeping the reef to your right, and the turret to your left, we pass to the beginning of the coral garden around 15m. With the coral garden at your right shoulder, you can now move north before following a bend in the garden to the south. Fine corals blanket this entire area and there are many caves and small caverns to look out for. The depth here is 10-15m, heading up to 2-5m. A weak current coming from the north affords excellent visibility. With the reef at your right shoulder you return to the mooring place of your boat.

ERG ABU DABAB

Drop-formed, this small reef is extended by a sharp end to the northeast. The depth is between 18-20m and the light currents give great visibility. It is best to dive on the external wall of the reef and the turrets to the southwest.

SHA'AB ABU DABBAB

This reef is one of the most remote from the coast. It is oval in shape and 500m long by 160m wide. At the northeast corner, the reef adjoins a large shallow plateau (80m long by 30-60m wide at 2-5m depth) that is joined to another reef. To the left of the plateau, there are a few sandy bays at 14-15m and a small connecting reef. To the right, small underwater mountains adjoin. The current runs here from north to south and is middle strength.

MARSA ABU DABBAB

This is a typical "marsa" being a coastal bay. The flat sandy bottom is covered with seagrass. The northern area is home to the moorings and also stingrays, lionfish and many other creatures. Tame octopus, squid and lots of large green turtles are all found here. Rare guitarfish also make an appearance.

The highlight of this dive site is the presence of the rare and unusual sea cow, the dugong. It is generally found grazing on the shallow sea grass, surrounded by a cloud of sand and silt as it munches its dinner. It is possible to begin the dive here via zodiac at the external part of the reef, coming back along the bay wall to the mooring place

---

sha'ab abu dabab, abou dabbab

Location:
32 km to north from Marsa Alam
25,5 km to south from Port Ghalib

GPS - position:
Abu Dabbab-2 (North)
25°20'51.96"N; 34°46'35.61" E
Abu Dabbab-3 (Gota)
25°20'42.81"N; 34°46'41.59" E

Access:
Safari, daily and speedboats

Mooring:
South extremities

Recommended level:
CMAS* / PADI OWD

Average depth:
12 m.

Maximum depth:
20 m.

Current:
Weak (1 knot and less)

Visibility:
Good (20-30 m)

Type of dives:
- Reef
- Wreck
- Fun

A great place to have a relaxing dive after Elphinstoun reef. A rough translation of the name is «Fathers Steps» or «Fathers' Stepping Stones». According to a legend, ancient gods stood in this place during an earthquake. Six fantastic reefs.

RSDASS — red sea association for diving & water sports

In 2002 in a province Red sea has been created the non-commercial, not state organization representing Diving and Water Sports community. The association aspires to improve the diving industry through marketing actions and technical support, protecting interests of all parties of process.

The purposes for creating of Association the following:
- Development and rationalization of an existing map of places of diving, for the purpose of increase in competitive appeal and environment preservation.
- Establishment, realization and support of standards of safety and quality for diving.
- Development and realization of all-round marketing and assistance to plans of increase in competitiveness of Red sea for tourism.
- Creation of the code of behavior for all operators in the diving industries and creation of insurance fund for professionals.
- Creation of the wide program of training for new shots of young competent professionals and modernization of quality and level already existing.
- Creation of information and communication centre for work with inquiries, problems, extreme situations, etc.
- Planning and the organization of internal and international exhibitions and actions.
- Advisory service for existing and potential operators and investors

Finally recognized as a primary source of revenue and tourism in the area, scuba diving gets a direct interest of official bodies such as the Governorate. The new standards aim to improve the quality and the level of service offered to visiting divers by the local operators, and are just a part of a bigger plan which will be implemented step by step in the near future.

Here a summary of the new regulations:
1. All scuba diving professionals operating in the Red Sea must prove their qualifications by obtaining a valid renewable Professional ID card from the Red Sea Association for Diving and Water sports.
2. No diving boat is allowed to operate without a qualified divemaster / instructor holding a valid RSDASS ID Card on board.
3. Divers with less than 25 logged dives MUST be accompanied in the water by a qualified divemaster / instructor holding a valid RSDASS ID Card, with a maximum ratio of 6 divers to 1 divemaster / instructor.
4. "Introductory dives" MUST be performed ONLY by qualified Instructors holding a valid RSDASS ID Card.
5. The maximum ratio in an introductory dive is of 2 guests to 1 instructor at the same time in the water.
6. Maximum depth for an introductory dive is 8 MSW.

On February 2005, Governor of the Red Sea approved suggestions by the Red Sea Association for modifications to rules dealing with safari and diving activities in the Red Sea:
1. Diving guest to guide ratio.
A- Marine Park safaris (Brothers, Zabargad, Daedalus, Rocky Island)
- One guide for a maximum of every eight diving guests.
- Minimum one crew member to be responsible for surface cover, such crew to be certified in O2 providing and MFA.
- Dive guides must have a valid Red Sea Association professional ID card.

B - NON Marine Park safaris.
- One guide for a maximum of every 12 (twelve) diving guests.
- A minimum of one crew member for surface cover, such member(s) to be certified in O2 providing and MFA.
- Dive guides must have a valid Red Sea Association professional ID card.

2. Prerequisites for diving guests for Marine Park safaris
- A minimum of 50 logged dives.
- A self declaration medical form duly signed by the diving guest.
- Valid insurance cover against diving accidents from a reputable company.

3. Prerequisites for diving guest for NON Marine Park safaris:
- No minimum number of logged dives required.
- Self declaration medical form duly signed by diving guest.
- Valid insurance cover against diving accidents by a reputable company.

4. Safety equipment for the safari dive guide (all safaris for Marine Park and NON Marine Park).
- Surface marker buoy.
- Strobe and torch.
- Mirror or similar light reflecting device.

5. Safety equipment for the safari diving guest (all safaris for Marine Park and NON Marine Park).
- Surface marker buoy.
- One torch for each buddy pair (in daytime dives).

6. Additional safety equipment for safari boats.
- A minimum of two binoculars on each safari boat for surface cover.
- A minimum of one zodiac on all safari boats (NON marine parks as well).
- Each safari boat (Marine Parks and NON Marine Park) must have a number of life rafts corresponding with the number of its passenger load.

7 - Daily diving rules (in addition to what is currently in place by dive centres such as medical form, liability release etc).
- One guide for every 12 certified divers (with 25 dives or more).
- One guide for every 8 beginners (less than 25 dives).
- Dive guides must have a valid Red Sea Association professional ID card.

For Information Contact
Tel. : 010 54 50 353 / 010 57 54 037
Red Sea Association for Diving & Watersports
Sheraton Road, opposite Marriot Hotel, Hurghada.
Tel. +20-65-444 802
Fax +20-65-444 801
E-mail: association@redseaexperience.com
Website: www.redseaexperience.com

HEPCA — hurghada environmental protection and conservation association

HEPCA is a Non Governmental Organization - registered with the Red Sea Governorate and established by members of the Red Sea diving community.

HEPCA'S mandate is the protection and conservation of the land and marine ecology and the underwater environment of the coral reefs, land ecosystems of the Red Sea and its coastline. Supported by its members and affiliated to governmental or non-governmental agencies, achieves its goals and objectives through active participation in all possible environmental projects and through other effective efforts. The spectacular coral reefs and fascinating marine life of the Red Sea are one of the main attractions for the 8 million visitors coming to Egypt each year. Dive tourism is booming here – divers and snorkels can choose from over 300 diving centers and boat operators in the Hurghada region alone.

Environmental deterioration is no longer a threat but a reality. Each day in the Red Sea we are witness to the depletion of the very resource base that attracts so many visitors here in the first place. Without proper environmental and logistical planning, and interventions to promote sustainable development, the corals and marine life of the Red Sea will die… affecting not only the environment, but hundreds of thousands of livelihoods, ultimately causing the degradation of the entire tourism industry along the Red Sea coast of Egypt.

The initiative to introduce reef protection in the Hurghada area took place in 1988 when the owners of four of the major dive centers met to discuss the problems associated with anchoring on the coral reefs. HEPCA was founded in 1992 by 12 members, representing the diving community of the Hurghada and Safaga region. The original objectives were expressed as the protection and conservation of marine ecology and the underwater environment of the Red Sea, and the promotion and improvement of diving safety. An initial mooring system was designed and installed, consisting of 100 mooring buoys, financed by private and public investment. Since these early days, the project has evolved into the largest mooring system in the world with over 1000 moorings installed and maintained throughout Hurghada, Safaga and the South.

In 1995 HEPCA was registered with the Red Sea Governorate and the Ministry of Social Affairs as a Non-Governmental – Non-Profit Making Organization. We are currently the leading NGO operating in Egypt in the field marine and land conservation. Our original objectives have grown and include other marine projects, such as underwater and beach clean-ups, and campaigns to stop over-fishing and protect endangered marine life.

HEPCA is also involved in a large number of projects concerning the local environment on land. We have instigated everything from training programs for local boat crews, to the development of solid waste management plants to help manage the vast amount of rubbish accumulated here. HEPCA is also involved in awareness raising activities targeted at the local community, schools, tourism industry, service providers, and visiting tourists.

HEPCA works closely with the Egyptian Environmental Affairs Agency (EEAA), Natural Protectorates Department, to ensure that laws covering the protection of all offshore islands and coral reefs are enforced, and to assist the Department in developing management and monitoring strategies. We are active in lobbying for legislation to protect our environment. Over the last 5 years, HEPCA has been at the forefront of campaigns, which have resulted in more than 32 laws, articles and decrees being changed.

As a non-profit making organization HEPCA would not be able to lead, and be involved in, as many projects as we do without the critical support and partnership of so many other organizations. HEPCA is supported by a huge network of members who assist with funding via membership fees and voluntary donations. The members nominate 11 individuals to represent them on the Board of Directors, who in turn give direction to HEPCA's Executive Director and support staff. Private funding from members and individuals is necessary for our survival but HEPCA is also fortunate to receive considerable funding from the public and private sector. Supporters include: the United States Agency for International Development (USAID); Coca Cola International, Vodafone Egypt International and many others.

HEPCA works closely a number of Government Departments including the Red Sea Governorate (RSG), the National Conservation Sector and the National Parks of Egypt and others. By supporting the work of HEPCA you can help ensure the preservation and sustainability of the Red Sea environment for future generations.

HEPCA needs your help in protecting the environment. Please keep your eyes and ears open and report any violations or disturbance of marine life to HEPCA. These include: fish feeding, dumping of garbage, fishing on dive sites, anchoring on the reef. HEPCA and its partners have the power to stop violators.

Contact HEPCA:
Marriott Hotel, Hurghada, Red Sea – Egypt
Tel: +20 65 344 5035
Fax: +20 65 344 6674
E-mail: info@hepca.com
Postal address: PO Box 104
Hurghada, Red Sea – Egypt HEPCA

PHONES useful

Emergency services

HURGHADA (065)
- Ambulance 3546490
- Decochamber 3549709
- Hospital «El Guna» 3580011
- Hospital «El Salam» 3548785
- General Hospital 3546740
- Military hospital 3549513
- Fire brigade 3549814
- Resque services 0122351313

SHARM EL SHEIKH (069)
- Ambulance 3600554
- Hospital «Sharm» 3661894
- Decochamber 3661011
- Fire brigade 3600633
- Clinic «Sinai Mount» 3601610
- Resque services 0123134158

Other services

HURGHADA (065)
- Airport 3442831
- Municipality 3546383
- Airline «Egypt Air» 3444365
- Flights information 3442831
- Money transfer 3442772
- Police 3546723
- Tourist police 3447773

SHARM EL SHEIKH (069)
- Airport 3601140
- Municipality 3660331
- Bus station 3660600
- Sea police 3600517
- Tourist police 3660675
- Sea Port 3660313

D.E.C.O. int. decompression chambers and medical emergencies network

EL GOUNA

Manufactured
HAUX Combi 2000 double lock HBO chamber
Germany

Date of manufacture: 1998

Date of installation 1998

Inner diameter 2 meters

Overall Length 4 meters

Capacity (main lock) 5 patients

Working Pressure: 5.5 bar

Location:
The chamber is located in El-Gouna hospital, 22 km north of Hurghada.
The hospital is a modern, with a very good team of doctors covering all specialties.
The chamber in El-Gouna treated more than 300 cases since starting of operation

Phone:
+20 65 3850 011-18
+20 12 7445 700

MARSA ALAM

Manufactured
Güssow double lock HBO chamber
Germany

Date of manufacture: 2007

Date of installation 20007

Inner diameter 2,1 meters

Overall Length 4 meters

Capacity: 8 patients

Working Pressure: 5,5 bar

Location:
15 KM south of Marsa Alam in Marsa Shagra Deco International Hyperbaric Medicine Center. The center is well equipped to deal adequately with both diving and non-diving related emergency situations.
The chamber has treated more than 200 cases since started operation.

Phone:
+20 122 190 383
+20 122 174 148

SAFAGA

Manufactured
Baromed DE 2000 Double locker
England

Date of manufacture: 2003

Date of installation 2003

Inner diameter 2 meters

Overall Length 4,75 meters

Capacity: 6 patients

Working Pressure: 6 bar

Location:
The chamber is located in the Deco International Hyperbaric Center in Safaga General Hospital.
The chamber has treated more than 50 cases since started operation

Phone:
+20 122 190 383
+20 121 741 533

Introduction	01-02
General map-scheme	03-04
Port Ghalib	05-06
Marsa Shona	07-08
Sha'ab Marsa Alam	09-10
Ras Torombi	11-12
Brothers Islands (general part)	13-14
Small Brother (general part)	15-16
Small Brother (northeast)	17-18
Small Brother (southwest)	19-20
Big Brother (southeast plateau)	21-22
Big Brother (Numidia)	23-24
Big Brother (Aida)	25-26
Daedalus	27-28
Rocky Island (general part)	29-30
Rocky (southwest)	31-32
Rocky (northeast)	33-34
Zabargad Island (south)	35-36
Zabargad Island (general part)	37-38
Saint Johns reef system (map-scheme)	40
Habili Ali	41-42
Habili Gafar	43-44
Abu Bassala	45-46
Dangerous	47-48
Gota Kebir	49-50
Gota Sogayar	51-52
Caves	53-54
Mikauwa	55-56
Fury Shoal reef system (map-scheme)	58
Sha'ab Maksour	59-60
Sha'ab Claudia	61-62
Malahi	63-64
Abu Galava	65-66
Sha'ab Sharm	67-68
Sha'ab Sharm (east plateau)	69
Sha'ab Sharm (west plateau)	70
Elphinestoun (north)	71-72
Elphinestoun (south)	73-74
Abu Dabbab	75-76
HEPCA (Hurghada Environmental Protection Association)	77
RSDASS (Red Sea Association for Diving & Water Sports)	77
Useful telephone & Decompression chambers DECO int.	78

RED SEA DIVE GUIDE

Andrei DVORETSKI © 2008
Hurghada, Red Sea, Egypt
+2 0114 364 1166
e-mail: info@r-divers.ru
web: www.r-divers.ru

Translation into English

Anna YUKHINA © 2008

Autors of photos:

Alexandr SHESTOPALETS © 2008
Hurghada, Red Sea, Egypt
+2 0122270067466
e-mail: sasha@aquadao.com
web: www.aquadao.com

Marina USTINOVA © 2008
Hurghada, Red Sea, Egypt
e-mail: marina@r-divers.ru
web: www.r-divers.ru

The information containing in the given book, is received by the author independently and checked up with the assistance of other local guides and the sources which are considered as the reliable. Nevertheless, meaning probable human or technical errors, the author cannot guarantee absolute accuracy and completeness of brought data and does not bear responsibility for the possible mistakes connected with use of the book.

Printed in Great Britain
by Amazon.co.uk, Ltd.,
Marston Gate.